Calypso Summer

Calypso Summer

Mike Coward

ABC
BOOKS

Every effort has been made to trace the original source of photographs in
this book. Where the attempt has been unsuccessful, the publishers would
be pleased to hear from the author/publisher to rectify any omission.

Published by ABC Books for the
AUSTRALIAN BROADCASTING CORPORATION
GPO Box 9994 Sydney NSW 2001

First published December 2000

National Library of Australia
Cataloguing-in-Publication data
Coward, Mike.
Calypso summer.
ISBN 0 7333 0886 4
1. Cricket – West Indies – History. 2. Cricket – Australia – History.
I. Australian Broadcasting Corporation. II. Title.
796.35865

Designed and typeset by Toni Hope-Caten
Set in 11pt/17pt New Baskerville
Film by PageSet, Victoria
Printed and bound in Singapore by Tien Wah Press

5   4   3   2   1

ACKNOWLEDGMENTS

It is always a challenge to find unpublished photographs of an event that captured the imagination of the nation as did the visit of Frank Worrell's West Indies cricket team to Australia in 1960-61.

How fortunate I was that friend David Studham at the splendid Melbourne Cricket Club Library recalled that a colleague and noted sports historian and author Alf Batchelder had some priceless images from the deciding fifth Test at the MCG in his private collection.

Now Alf's photographs are to be widely seen, and I am most grateful to him. Bernard Whimpress, the curator of the museum at Adelaide Oval, has generously consented to the publication of amateur photographer Albert Devonshire's splendid shot of Lance Gibbs' famous hat-trick ball in the fourth Test at Adelaide.

The image is rare, as it was taken from square with the wicket. Devonshire's nephew Darren Silva recently ensured that the photograph reached Whimpress.

I'm also in debt to Jim Coulter, who fossicked through family albums to find a delightful photograph of his dear friend Sir Conrad Hunte coaching boys in a Melbourne park in the 1960s and Alan Davidson who parted momentarily with the precious tie tack commissioned by Sir Donald Bradman for those who played in the game's first tied Test match.

And good friends and great shooters Trent Parke (Sydney) and Gordon Brooks (Bridgetown, Barbados), along with Stuart Hannagan at Allsport and Rick Smith, also helped significantly along the way.

My thanks also to Jillanne (JJ) Martin, who made life more manageable with precise transcriptions of many hours of taped interviews and, as ever, to Ernie Cosgrove, Ross Dundas and Charles Davis, who produced the relevant statistics.

Finally, to Matthew Kelly, publisher at ABC books, and his colleague Stuart Neal, who quickly saw the merit of a conjunction with the television documentary and enthusiastically set the wheels in motion.

Mike Coward
Sydney, June 2000

DEDICATION

To the memory of Sir Frank Worrell, Sir Conrad Hunte,
Wally Grout, Ken Mackay, Les Favell and Johnny Martin

Contents

Paying homage. Thousands of sated fans crowd on to the Melbourne Cricket Ground for the unveiling of the Frank Worrell Trophy on February 15, 1961. *News Ltd*

Author's Note

Given the darkness that has descended on cricket recently, there is an urgent need to reaffirm the game's truest values and richest traditions.

This can be simply and happily accomplished by revisiting the most significant Test series of the modern era — the five matches between Australia and the West Indies in 1960–61 that gave rise to the Frank Worrell Trophy.

Calypso Summer, published to complement the television documentary of the same name, is a tribute to distinguished cricketers of an island continent on one side of the world and an exotic archipelago on the other, who so selflessly and thrillingly gave new life to Test cricket.

The cricket played was exceptional. The leadership of Frank Worrell and Richie Benaud was exceptional. And the spirit in which the series was played was exceptional. Unique, actually.

As West Indian batsman Peter Lashley observed, it was 'a very beautiful series of cricket'.

The matches were played by mates and watched by men, women and children who wanted to be their mates.

It was a glorious celebration of an ancient game in a modern world daring to change.

For those of us who made our first raucous appeals in the baby boom that followed World War II, the summer of 1960–61 was filled with great joy. None of us wanted it to end and all of us have special memories of it.

I can still sense the excitement and smell the nervousness of sitting next to the white picket fence in front of the scoreboard at Adelaide Oval on 1 February 1961 as Ken Mackay and Lindsay Kline gallantly defied the West Indian attack for an eternity. For a moment I even forgot that Les Favell, my summer god, had been out for four the previous night in the last of his 19 Tests. But at least he hooked and cut to the very last.

So I was delighted when passionate producer-writer Lincoln Tyner asked me to conduct the interviews for the television documentary about the series.

Neil Harvey (left) and Norm O'Neill make their way through young faithful after an unbroken stand of 99 for the third wicket at Sydney on January 17, 1961. *News Ltd*

It was a joy to talk to these men about a summer of such goodwill and affection and to learn of the depth of their friendships forged 40 years ago. At the same time it filled me with great regret that I never had the privilege of meeting Sir Frank Worrell. It said a great deal about Worrell that the members of his team I interviewed mostly spoke of him in the present tense.

Sir Conrad Hunte took a keen interest in Calypso Summer, but sadly did not live to see its completion. Suffice it to say the contribution of this wonderful, wise and loving man was beyond compare.

The series had a profound impact on many people, and undeniably ignited a passion for the game in a generation, both in the international cricket community and beyond.

If cricket today can rekindle the spirit and feeling of the summer of 1960–61, some of the darkness will lift and we can again talk of the game with pride and watch it being celebrated with joy.

The Players

Australia

Richie Benaud (NSW) Captain. b Penrith, NSW, 6 October 1930. 63 Tests, 2201 runs @ 24.45, 248 wickets @ 27.03. Captained Australia in 28 matches.

Neil Harvey (NSW) Vice-Captain. b. Fitzroy, Victoria, 8 October 1928. 79 Tests, 6149 runs @48.41. Captained Australia in one Test.

Peter Burge (QLD) b Buranda, Queensland 17 May 1932. 42 Tests, 2290 runs @38.16.

Alan Davidson (NSW) b Lisarow, NSW, 14 June 1929. 44 Tests, 1328 runs @ 24.59, 186 wickets @ 20.53.

Les Favell (SA) b Arncliffe, NSW, 6 October 1929, d Adelaid 14 June1987. 19 Tests, 757 runs @ 27.03.

Wally Grout (Qld) b Mackay, Queensland, 30 March 1927, d Brisbane 9 November 1968. 51 Tests, 890 runs @ 15.08, 187 dismissals, 163 caught, 24 stumped.

Des Hoare (WA) b Perth, Western Australia, 19 October 1934. One Test, 35 runs @ 17.50, 2 wickets @ 78.00.

LINDSAY KLINE (Vic) b Camberwell, Victoria, 29 September 1934. 13 Tests, 58 runs @ 8.28, 34 wickets @ 22.82.

COLIN McDONALD (Vic) b Glen Iris, Victoria 17 November 1928. 47 Tests, 3197 runs @ 39.32.

KEN MACKAY (Qld) b Windsor, Queensland, 24 October 1925, d Stradbroke Island, Queensland, 13 June 1982. 37 Tests, 1507 runs @ 33.48, 50 wickets @ 29.78.

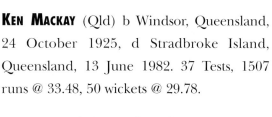

JOHNNY MARTIN (NSW) b Wingham, NSW 28 July 1931, d Werris Creek, NSW 16 July 1992. 8 Tests, 214 runs @ 17.83, 17 wickets @ 48.94.

IAN MECKIFF (Vic) b Mentone, Victoria 6 January 1935. 18 Tests, 154 runs @ 11.84, 45 wickets @ 31.62.

FRANK MISSON b Darlinghurst, NSW, 19 November 1938. Five Tests, 38 runs @ 19.00, 16 wickets @ 38.50.

NORMAN O'NEILL (NSW) b Carlton, NSW, 19 February 1937. 42 Tests, 2779 runs @ 45.55.

BOB SIMPSON (NSW) b Marrickville, NSW, 3 February 1936. 62 Tests, 4869 runs @ 46.81, 71 wickets @ 42.26, 110 catches. Captained Australia in 39 Tests.

THE PLAYERS

West Indies

FRANK WORRELL (Jamaica) Captain. b Bridgetown, Barbados, 1 August 1924, d Kingston, Jamaica, 13 May 1967. 51 Tests, 3860 runs @ 49.48, 69 wickets @, 38.72. Captained West Indies in 15 Tests.

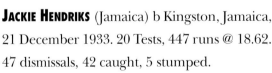

GERRY ALEXANDER (Jamaica) Vice-Captain. b Kingston, Jamaica, 2 November 1928. 25 Tests, 961 runs @ 30.03, 90 dismissals, 85 caught, 5 stumped. Captained West Indies in 18 Tests.

TOM DEWDNEY (Jamaica) b Kingston, Jamaica, 23 October 1933. 9 Tests, 17 runs @ 2.47, 21 wickets @ 38.42.

LANCE GIBBS (Guyana) b Georgetown, Guyana, 29 September 1934. 79 Tests, 488 runs @ 6.97, 309 wickets @ 29.09.

WES HALL (Barbados) b Christchurch, Barbados, 12 September 1937. 48 Tests, 818 runs @ 15.73, 192 wickets @ 26.38.

JACKIE HENDRIKS (Jamaica) b Kingston, Jamaica, 21 December 1933. 20 Tests, 447 runs @ 18.62. 47 dismissals, 42 caught, 5 stumped.

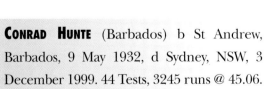

CONRAD HUNTE (Barbados) b St Andrew, Barbados, 9 May 1932, d Sydney, NSW, 3 December 1999. 44 Tests, 3245 runs @ 45.06.

ROHAN KANHAI (Guyana) b Berbice, Guyana, 26 December 1935. 79 Tests, 6227 runs @ 47.53. Captained West Indies in 13 Tests.

CHESTER WATSON (Jamaica) b Westmoreland, Jamaica, 1 July 1938. 7 Tests, 12 runs @ 2.40, 19 wickets @ 38.34.

SEYMOUR NURSE (Barbados) b Bridgetown, Barbados, 10 November 1933. 29 Tests, 2523 runs @ 47.60.

PETER LASHLEY (Barbados) b Christchurch, Barbados, 11 February 1937. 4 Tests, 159 runs @ 22.71.

CAMMIE SMITH (Barbados) b Christchurch, Barbados, 29 July 1933. 5 Tests, 222 runs @ 24.66.

SONNY RAMADHIN (Trinidad) b Esperance Village, Trinidad, 1 May 1929. 43 Tests, 361 runs @ 8.20. 158 wickets @ 28.98.

JOE SOLOMON (Guyana) b Berbice, Guyana, 26 August 1930. 27 Tests, 1326 runs @ 34.00.

GARFIELD SOBERS (Barbados) b Bridgetown, Barbados, 28 July 1936. 93 Tests, 8032 runs @ 57.78. 235 wickets @ 34.03. Captained West Indies in 39 Tests.

ALF VALENTINE (Jamaica) b Kingston, Jamaica, 29 April 1930. 36 Tests, 141 runs @ 4.70, 139 wickets @ 30.32.

Iconic image. Ian Meckiff is brilliantly run out by Joe Solomon and for the first time in 502 matches over 83 years a Test is tied. *Ron Lovitt/Age*

A VERY BEAUTIFUL SERIES OF CRICKET

The doomsayers who are periodically drawn to Test cricket were especially strident during the latter stages of the 20th century.

Their voices grew progressively louder as a game so rich in history and tradition succumbed to the commercial imperative and was steadily consumed by the unsatisfying, mostly unmemorable and, evidently, corrupt one-day form of the game. They contended that the pure game — or long game, as it so crassly became known — was an anachronistic legacy of a vanished Empire and of little relevance in the game's brave new world.

It was not, however, the tumult ignited by the 1977 World Series Cricket revolution, the defining event of the modern game, that first gave the pessimists and heretics a major platform and a chance to be heard.

The 1950s are often portrayed as an uninspiring and unimaginative period partitioning the grim, tumultuous 1940s from the carefree, liberating 1960s.

While some historians and social commentators believe the 1950s deserve a more generous appreciation, Test cricket of the time was unquestionably uninspiring and unimaginative. Certainly John Arlott, the doyen of cricket broadcasters and writers, saw no reason to alter his contention that at any given time the game generally reflects the moods and mores of the wider community.

At the close of the 1950s not even Sir Donald Bradman, the most influential cricket person of the 20th century, could mask his fears for the future welfare of Test cricket.

Despite Australia's emphatic 4–0 success and the emergence of Richie Benaud as an exceptional leader, the 1958–59 Ashes series was often a turgid affair, and it did little to ease the disquiet of the Australian cricket community.

Nor was it an isolated event. England's tour of the Caribbean in 1959–60 produced four draws in five Tests, and such mindlessly tedious cricket that West Indies captain Gerry Alexander seriously considered bringing forward his retirement to concentrate on work at his veterinary practice in Jamaica.

His dissatisfaction with the game was intense, and many of his colleagues felt the same way.

Cricket was being endured, not celebrated, and spectators hankered for the joyous game played in England by Australia in 1948 and by the West Indies in 1950. It had become a game of attrition, with England, especially, more intent on ensuring that they did not lose rather than determinedly trying to win. Furthermore, it was blighted by wickedly slow over-rates and vexed controversies surrounding 'throwing' and 'dragging'.

There was an urgent need for change; and the game was fortunate in having, at this time, the calibre of men who could effect major change and carry the new standard to the world.

Renowned for his clarity of thought and practicalness, Sir Donald was convinced that a series of exceptional enterprise and entertainment would reinvigorate Test cricket and re-engage the people. To this end he enlisted the services of Benaud, whom he knew to be a friend and admirer of Frank Worrell. Worrell, to the undisguised relief of the international cricket community, had finally been appointed captain of the West Indies team.

Worrell's appointment represented change on a massive scale. He was the first black man to lead the West Indies outside the Caribbean since they entered the Test match arena at Lord's in June 1928.

Furthermore, Sir Donald knew that Worrell had spent much of the latter part of the 1950s at University in Manchester, England, and so had been spared the tedium that had beset the game. He would be ripe for a challenge, reasoned Sir Donald.

It is unclear whether or not Sir Donald directly appealed to Worrell. However, as chairman of the then Australian Board of Control for International Cricket (renamed the Australian Cricket Board in 1973) and a selector, he was regularly in close proximity

The mastermind and his disciples. Sir Donald Bradman (right) who called upon captains Richie Benaud and Frank Worrell to play with enterprise and reignite public interest in Test match cricket.
Alf Batchelder

21

to the visitors, and so was presented with many opportunities to chat informally with the West Indies captain and management.

Suffice it to say that Benaud was happy to conscript Worrell to the cause, and together they oversaw a series that set a benchmark, and is still spoken about with undiminished enthusiasm 40 years later.

And the measure of excellence was not confined to the standard of play. The matches were played in a spirit of friendship and mutual respect — even affection — largely beyond the comprehension of those who have succeeded them.

It was a season of goodwill that brought great pleasure to the protagonists and the people. It was of even greater importance to Conrad Hunte and Alf Valentine. Their lives were to be transformed by the Australian experience.

The game has not seen the like before or since.

SIR GARFIELD SOBERS: The kind of cricket that was played on that tour — I don't think I've ever seen it played before or after. I don't think there will be another series like that 1960–61 series. On and off the field we had a magnificent relationship with the players and the Australian people. Wherever we went we were loved.

ALAN DAVIDSON: To us it was unforgettable. Out of all the series we ever played, there was never a series where there was such incredible cricket.

Such was the significance of the series and its impact on the entire cricket world that Sir Donald sought the approval of his board to create the Frank Worrell Trophy for future competition between the teams. The trophy was unveiled at an emotional presentation ceremony at the Melbourne Cricket Ground on 15 February 1961.

At the dawn of the 21st century, the trophy has gained even greater sheen, and with England's fall from grace and influence it has supplanted the Ashes as the game's most prestigious prize.

Three times the inaugural Frank Worrell Trophy series brought Australia to a halt, just as the Melbourne Cup has done each year since 1861.

The opening Test in Brisbane produced the first tie in 498 Tests over 83 years and the fourth, in Adelaide, saw Australia's last batsmen, Ken Mackay and Lindsay Kline, defy the might of the West Indian attack for 110 minutes to achieve an improbable draw. In the end, the series was decided 2–1 in Australia's favour by two wickets in a nerve-racking and controversial final match in Melbourne that attracted a crowd of 90,800 on one day.

Even those not especially enamoured of the game were caught up in the excitement of the series and followed it avidly.

PETER LASHLEY: The people, the umpires, cricketers all got caught up in a series that began with a tied Test and set the stage for a very beautiful series of cricket.

A remarkable number of the people who can nominate where they were when they learned of the assassination of US president John Kennedy in 1963 and the drowning of Australian prime minister Harold Holt in 1966 can also nominate their whereabouts when the Test was tied at Brisbane on 14 December 1960.

It was a moment in time.

In a thorough account of the West Indies visit in his tour book, *With the West Indies in Australia 1960–61*, renowned broadcaster AG 'Johnnie' Moyes wrote of the conclusion in Brisbane:

Benaud came through the gate on to the field of honour to shake Worrell by the hand and we saw the two captains who had conspired together to make cricket a game once again; two captains who spurned the idea of playing for a draw [and] who now rejoiced, I am sure, that they had breathed new life into the dead bones of a game which had been starved to death by indecisive batting, lack of inspiration in bowling, dullness

Distinguished cricket commentator, newspaperman and author Alban George 'Johnnie' Moyes who travelled the length and breadth of the country with the West Indies and broadcast the series for the ABC. Moyes who played first-class cricket for South Australia and Victoria is seen with peerless fast bowler Ray Lindwall, a co-commentator at the time. *ABC*

The power of an ancient game. Dr Barton Babbage, the Dean of Melbourne. *News Ltd*

and lack of adventure in leadership. We thanked them, some of us silently, as we looked down from the broadcasting box, and some with cheers as they stood in front of the dressingrooms to pay their allegiance to those who had caused their hearts to leap in loyalty.

While the ranks of those who intimately recall the series diminish with the passing of every summer, the eyewitness accounts and memories so happily bequeathed provide priceless evidence of an unforgettable time in the annals of the game.

IAN MECKIFF: The West Indies really attracted the people and probably did more for cricket than any other side.

The 1960s were characterised by change, with the very word becoming something of a mantra to the so-called 'baby boomer' generation in Australia. Again, the game mirrored moods beyond the boundary.

Change in the Caribbean was profound, and Worrell's belated appointment to the leadership was made to a backdrop of great political and social activism as the fledgling West Indies Federation endeavoured to strike a chord of unity in the region. The reality, however, did not match the rhetoric, and after four years the federation was disbanded, in 1962.

But its failure in no way slowed the march of the island nations in the sun towards independence. In time they were rid of their colonial cloaks — Jamaica and Trinidad and Tobago in 1962 and Barbados and British Guiana (now Guyana) on the South American mainland in 1966.

While the people of the Caribbean had reason for optimism, the black minority in Australia continued to suffer institutionalised discrimination and were numbered among the world's most disadvantaged people.

To the unease of civil libertarians, social reformers and some church leaders, Australians who were unaware of or indifferent to the plight of Aboriginal people embraced the West Indians with unabashed vigour.

Dr Barton Babbage, the Dean of St Paul's Anglican Cathedral Melbourne, seized upon the extraordinary popularity of the West Indian team to address wider issues during a sermon he delivered during the fifth and final Test match at Melbourne:

It is a sobering and humbling thought that the West Indians whom Australia welcomes as cricketers would not be welcome as citizens. Their skin is the wrong colour. They may play with us, but they may not stay with us. It may be that the game of cricket will pave the way for more generous national policies. If only we could cultivate the spirit of cricket in all our dealings, one with the other. It is not far from the spirit of Christ.

While the Federal Council for the Advancement of Aborigines and Torres Strait Islanders (FCAATSI) was set up in 1957, it was to be another 10 years before the referendum which saw the Australian people overwhelmingly end the constitutional discrimination against Aborigines.

The predominantly black West Indies team were aware of Australia's iniquitous White Australia Policy and the newcomers in the party sought assurance from Worrell, Alf Valentine and Sonny Ramadhin, the survivors of John Goddard's tour nine years earlier, that they would not be racially taunted or made to feel unwelcome.

ALF VALENTINE: Australia was much different; more relaxed. People were much more friendly and would want an invite to your hotel and things like that. In 1951 we travelled more in a group, and I believe we used to have some passbooks with our photograph in it. I blew into a club somewhere in Sydney and had to show some ID. In 1960 you could move around and everyone knew you were with the West Indies team. I went and visited people I'd met in 1951; in fact I spent Christmas privately.

GERRY ALEXANDER: There was an occasion when we were invited for lunch by a lady and three of us went to lunch. She informed us that really and truly, it was because we were VIP cricketers that she would have us in her house. But she would not have the Aboriginals in her house, black people in her house, because that was not the way she was brought up and she would not feel comfortable.

Certainly there was a greater worldliness within the Australian team, which had travelled far and wide over the previous five years. In addition to traditional visits to England in 1956 and South Africa in 1957–58, they made pioneering tours of the West Indies in 1954–55 and Pakistan and India in 1956 and again in 1959–60.

COLIN McDONALD: The West Indies players must have come here with some mixed emotions, in that Australia still had a White Australia policy and they were largely a team of black men. They must have wondered what sort of reception they were going to get. I think it was a proud year for the Australian people. They did throw away any racial tendencies they may have had.

If the West Indians reached Australia with any preconceived notions, they were anxious not to show them.

Indeed, it was evident soon enough that under Worrell's leadership the West Indian players were more relaxed than often had been the case when they were away from the familiarity of the Caribbean.

Furthermore, there was, too, a oneness, a rare sense of family within the touring party. In a remarkably short space of time Worrell broke down the inter-island jealousies and rivalries and, perhaps for the first time, promoted a true sense of the Caribbean collective. To this end it was most appropriate that the team played under the banner of the infant West Indies Federation.

One of Worrell's most conspicuous and influential supporters was the noted West Indian writer and activist CLR James, who so famously asked in his acclaimed book *Beyond a Boundary:* What do they know of cricket who only cricket know?

It was a question that resonated with Worrell, and to some extent underpinned his philosophy as a leader. His vision extended well beyond the boundary, and he was determined that his team would advance the cause of the black man on the world stage. To this end, acceptance of umpiring decisions without complaint was of paramount performance. It was a fundamental tenet and rigidly enforced.

It is unlikely that there has ever been a more disciplined touring team in Australia.

CLR James, historian, social analyst and literary master who so memorably observed: What do they know of cricket who only cricket know?
Steve Pyke

WES HALL: Frank clearly understood that we were a bunch of good individual cricketers, and his dream was that West Indies should be known as a cohesive force. He thought Australia was a great place to do it. You were there for six months, you were in happy and congenial surroundings and he thought that socially we'd be OK. There had to be a transformation of our lives, our cricketing lives, and a renewing of our minds as we looked at the game. In other words, there had to be a mindset that was so much different from being a calypso cricketer. So I think that was the big thing with Worrell. I think he understood it perfectly.

SIR CONRAD HUNTE: He told us we were not just flannel fools, not just cricketers, but statesmen. We not only must uphold the West Indies' standing as cricket-playing countries but must establish a West Indies identity which would be respected and admired by the rest of the world. It was therefore going to depend on us not just as players but as diplomats to make that image permanent; make it something worthwhile in the world at large. It (the White Australia policy) was never talked about, but we knew that they had to pass certain regulation changes for us to go there and to be admitted on a par with everyone else. I think this must have impinged on Frank and his thinking and that is why, I think, he was so insistent that we deserved and merited the appreciation and response, [the] positive response of Australian people.

Not in his wildest dreams could Worrell have imagined the positiveness of the response of the Australian people. Men, women and children, especially adolescents, embraced the West Indians with a fervour not before seen in Australian cricket — perhaps not before seen in Australian sport, save for the Olympic Games in Melbourne in 1956.

While the exotic nature of the West Indians surely accounted for some of this fascination — it was, after all, only the third visit by the West Indies to Australia in 30 years — they were also openly loved for their extraordinary abilities and natural athleticism and their exceptional sportsmanship.

Even given the distinctively Australian trait of supporting the underdog, the number of Australians who upset some of the Australian players by overtly supporting the West Indies was extraordinary.

In Melbourne during the second Test the support for the West Indians manifested itself in the loud and sustained booing of Benaud after he declined to call back Joe Solomon, who had been bowled when his cap fell on his stumps.

That Solomon was out under the laws of the game and Benaud had acted strictly within his rights did not appease the crowd.

This outpouring of emotion by the Australian people reached a climax on 17 February 1961 when a crowd estimated at 500,000 lined Collins and Swanston streets in Melbourne to farewell the West Indies as they were driven in beribboned convertibles to a civic reception at the Town Hall.

When the players appeared on the Town Hall balcony to take a bow — like royalty or pop stars — the people waved enthusiastically, unselfconsciously threw streamers and confetti and cheered themselves hoarse.

Many of the West Indian players wore sunglasses which not only served to deflect the glare of the sun and the flashlights of cameras but also concealed the tears of pride which flowed freely.

Auld lang syne. A half a million people gathered in Melbourne on February 17, 1961 to farewell a West Indian team that had won the hearts of the nation. *Age*

COLIN McDONALD: They didn't look at the colour of their skins — the Australian people loved the West Indians because of the way they played cricket. And they were obviously gentlemen. Frank Worrell picked that up and he realised they were loved and I think the emotion got to him.

ALF VALENTINE: Frank [Worrell] cried; cried like a baby. He was accepted. I think so.

ALAN DAVIDSON: I think the West Indians got a hell of a shock themselves to think that that's what the people of Australia thought of them. I don't think in their wildest dreams they ever imagined they were sort of demigods to everybody.

JACKIE HENDRIKS: I think every one of us, without exception, was so deeply touched. I don't think you ever forget that sort of outpouring of love, and [the] feeling that we seemed to have done something for Australian crowds and for cricket.

They may have lost the series, but as the Melbourne press observed, the West Indians had won the hearts of the Australian people.

In his review of the tour 'Johnnie' Moyes wrote:

Those who had the pleasure of watching the West Indian cricketers in action and of knowing them personally will never forget them. The impact they made on cricket in Australia was amazing: they turned the world upside down; they arrived almost unhonoured and unsung; they took away with them the esteem, affection and admiration of all sections of the community. They gave the genuine cricket lover a thrill he had not felt for a quarter of a century. They brought back to the grounds many who had left them in disgust at the mediocre fare served up to them. They proved what so many of us had declared — that people would go to see cricket played as a game and an entertainment.

Furthermore, it was a game and an entertainment provided by mates. For all the intensity of the rivalries in the middle, the closeness of the protagonists off the field was unparalleled.

For some, the series provided an opportunity to reminisce.

Six of the 15 Australians called to duty had toured the Caribbean in 1955 and had fond memories of their journey. Similarly, five members of the West Indian team of 1955 had survived to make the trip to Australia.

Furthermore, in 1951–52 Neil Harvey was emerging as one of Australia's greatest batsmen when Benaud and Colin McDonald made their Test debut in Sydney against Worrell, Valentine and Ramadhin.

While old acquaintances were renewed, new friendships were quickly and easily forged before the Test matches had even begun. Lindsay Kline can recall five or six of the Australians with five or six of the West Indian players listening to calypso records in Garfield Sobers' room at Lennons Hotel, Brisbane the night before the first Test match.

The next day Sobers flayed the Australian bowlers for one of the greatest centuries in the history of Test cricket. Nevertheless, along with Sir Donald Bradman, the Australians were among the first to warmly congratulate him at the end of the day.

CONRAD HUNTE: We were in and out of each other's dressing-grooms all the time. Even though we fought hard on the field, we were mates off the field, and I think that added to the whole camaraderie, the whole spirit of the tour, which I think became a benchmark for all future tours Down Under, no question.

ALF VALENTINE: After you came off the field everybody got together, and some of the boys would come over and talk with us. The captain, Richie Benaud, was always coming around saying 'Hi, Frank [Worrell], how's so and so', and they're talking and the relationship was great between both teams.

Often the players socialised together at the hotels the cricket board had designated for both teams. On other occasions they would go together to the cinema and private parties or, if Valentine had his way, to a jazz club. Valentine was introduced to jazz by Sir Everton Weekes in 1950, and remains an aficionado, with an impressive private collection. To Valentine's delight, a group of Australia jazz musicians who occasionally toured Jamaica were on home duty the summer of 1960–61.

Those with a predilection for a wager were often seen in the company of Alan Davidson and heading for the trots at Harold Park in Sydney or at other paceways and racetracks around the country. Invariably, the irrepressible Wes Hall and the ever-laughing Cammie Smith would be with Davidson.

Benaud and Worrell were prepared to allow their men full rein, provided they remained mindful of their responsibilities and were mentally and physically fit and willing on match days. They were leaders of men and led accordingly.

Attempts by players and critics of the day to make a comparative study of the captains achieved little. Even those who thought Benaud had been the more imaginative and attacking were unstinting in their praise of Worrell's generalship and his capacity to unite his troops.

Given the significance of the series to the welfare of Test cricket everywhere, the nit-picking was needless.

Suffice it to say that the game remains in the debt of these men.

So effective was Worrell in creating a sense of family, and so homely and welcoming was the Australian environment, that Hall, Sobers, Rohan Kanhai and Lance Gibbs happily returned to Australia to play Sheffield Shield cricket. Hall represented Queensland in 1961–62 and 1962–63, Sobers played for South Australia for three consecutive seasons from 1961–62, and Kanhai played for Western Australia in 1961–62 and then Tasmania in 1969–70, the same season that Gibbs appeared in South Australian colours.

Worrell's shrewd counselling and cajoling of Hall and restraining, almost parental guiding of Sobers was matched by Benaud's consummate management of his ace all-rounder Davidson.

While the Australians seriously but quietly doubted Worrell's judgment in overlooking paceman Chester Watson for all but the second Test match, thereby burdening himself with new-ball duties at the age of 36, they appreciated his skilful deployment of Sobers.

Under Worrell's predecessors, Sobers had occupied each batting position from number one to nine, where he had made his debut ahead of only Frank King and Sonny Ramadhin against England in 1953.

Jamaican Chester Watson who to the surprise of many Australian players and critics was overlooked for four of the five Test matches. *ABC*

Kanhai was also a batsman of formidable ability, but Worrell considered Sobers the most mature of his batsmen, and from four, five or six, in the best position to judge the state of the innings and play accordingly. He had the necessary skills to attack ruthlessly or defend responsibly but productively.

Sobers' magnificent hundreds in Brisbane and Sydney, crafted at four, were two of five centuries the West Indies scored in the series. Kanhai completed the rare distinction of scoring a century in each innings of the Adelaide Test, and vice-captain and redoubtable keeper-batsman Gerry Alexander recorded his maiden first-class hundred in the third Test at Sydney.

Given that Australia won the series, it was remarkable Norm O'Neill, with a glorious 181, was their only century scorer. Bob Simpson (twice) and Colin McDonald returned scores in the 90s.

If Hall and Sobers were Worrell's trumps, then Davidson was Benaud's.

Friends and both opponents and team-mates since their high school days Benaud was an outstanding captain for Davidson who, for all his greatness, was given to well-documented moments of hypochondria. Benaud understood Davidson's foibles and made light of them. He also knew better than most the size of Davidson's heart and the extent of his commitment to cause and country.

Clarrie Grimmett, the incomparable, wily Fox who set the benchmark with 33 wickets against the West Indies in 1930-31. *ABC*

They were regarded among the world's elite all-rounders following their stunning successes on the exceptionally happy tour of South Africa under 22-year-old captain Ian Craig in 1957–58, and between them held the key to Australia's fortunes in the series.

Indeed, the comradeship that so characterised Benaud's distinguished teams had its genesis on that South African tour. Richie Benaud:

Our planning with Davo was to set a whole line of slips and have our third man very square. This would allow Davo to keep the ball right up to the bat all the time. I would give him some cover at mid-off but no one at mid-on, because he was going to cover that himself. For the right-handers Davo would keep the ball up at driving length and take the risk of being smashed all over the park, and we would have the benefit of being able to pick up catches. And we had a wonderful slips catching cordon. And he hardly bowled a short ball. That was the tactic — to attack and give the batsman the opportunity to smash it all over the park.

Despite missing the Adelaide Test with a hamstring injury, Davidson equalled Clarrie Grimmett's 1930–31 record of 33 wickets for a home series with the West Indies. It's a record they still hold. Astonishingly, 15 of keeper Wally Grout's 20 catches for the series — together with three stumpings — came from Davidson's bowling. Grout did not complete a dismissal in Davidson's absence in Adelaide.

The commitment to excellence and a better cricket world by leaders of the stature of Worrell and Benaud gave the series a distinctive atmosphere.

Davidson still can't find the appropriate words to explain the depth of the relationship between the two teams and the indescribable aura created by the series.

LINDSAY KLINE: And the press picked it up too; and the public did. They could feel something special.

While the series gave rise to the intense rivalry that is now a feature of all matches between Australia and the West Indies, there is no longer any sentimental attachment between the teams.

To the deep distress of those who shared the joy of the 1960–61 series, the mutual respect and mateship evaporated four years later in the Caribbean, when opposing captains Sobers and Simpson were often at loggerheads and debate raged about the legitimacy of the bowling action of fast bowler Charlie Griffith.

Wally Grout: His country's keeper.
ABC

The Worrell headstone at the University of the West Indies campus, Cave Hill outside Bridgetown, Barbados. *Mike Coward*

In the circumstances, Worrell, who was team manager of Sobers' team, must have been consumed by mixed emotions. While the West Indies triumphed 2–1, it seemed much of the joy of the contest had been extinguished.

But mercifully Worrell saw the trophy that had been named in his honour in the hands of the Caribbean people before his death from leukemia in March 1967. He was 42.

IAN MECKIFF: He was just one of those beautiful men.

There was a time when Australian teams made a pilgrimage to the grave of Worrell at the University of the West Indies campus outside Bridgetown, Barbados, laid a wreath and paused for reflection. Similarly, there was a time when West Indies teams would visit the grave of Victor Trumper at Waverley Cemetery, Sydney, and lay a wreath and pause for reflection.

Disappointingly, the contemporary cricketer does not seem to have time to pause or to reflect.

With some notable exceptions at the time Ian and Greg Chappell had charge, the ill-tempered, controversial exchange of 1965 set the tenor for future series, with the visit of Allan Border's team in 1991 being particularly acrimonious. Time and again grudges, prejudices and jealousies have been carried over from one series to the next.

To some extent the ever-present drama and controversy of Worrell Trophy matches can be attributed to the toughness and gut-wrenching intensity of competition.

Since the tied Test match at Brisbane there have been 74 Worrell Trophy matches — the West Indies have won 29, Australia 26, and 19 have been drawn. Yet for all the angst and uneasiness, there remains a professional respect and mutual appreciation of capability and ambition, even if the affection has vanished.

Much like India, Pakistan and Sri Lanka, the West Indies cricket community has long been influenced by the Australian game and the philosophy and approach of its elite players.

That the West Indies dominated world cricket throughout the 1980s and into the mid-1990s was, to some degree, the result of observations made and lessons learned in Australia in 1960–61 and again, at Clive Lloyd's urging, during the World Series Cricket revolution in the late 1970s.

These were the seminal times in the modern history of West Indies cricket, and whatever the state of the game throughout the Caribbean, in a rapidly changing world Worrell will forever be the spirit of cricket between Australia and the West Indies.

Portrait of a champion. Frank Mortimore Maglinne Worrell, the spirit of cricket between Australia and the West Indies. *News Ltd*

CONRAD HUNTE: Frank's impact on the West Indies people first, and West Indies cricket, is eternal. He saw in these islands of ours the need for what I call a collective cohesiveness — a dynamic one that is shown in our cricket. But that's only a mirror. It also has to take place politically and economically in these wonderful islands of ours. His mark both in cricket and with the West Indies people is that of a prophet who saw ahead of his time what was needed and set it in place. And his leadership was such that it survived him to Garry Sobers, Clive Lloyd and Viv Richards.

The greatest challenge for impressive, thoughtful Jimmy Adams is to

Steve Waugh, following in the footsteps of Richie Benaud.
Right: Jimmy Adams, following in the footsteps of Frank Worrell.
Patrick Eagar

rekindle the spirit of Worrell in his emerging West Indies team as competition for the Worrell Trophy enters the 21st century.

To this end Adams' counterpart, Steve Waugh, is more fortunate. He has access to the vast reservoir of knowledge stored by Benaud, who at the age of 70 remains the game's foremost broadcaster and critic and natural successor to Sir Donald Bradman as the eminence grise of Australian cricket.

And while he would never impose himself or his philosophy on any Australian captain or team, if asked for an opinion he will answer quietly and wisely.

RICHIE BENAUD: Frank's legacy is the fact that cricket became a better game in that particular series and from the things he did. You always need a captain to leave a legacy of some kind. And Worrell left one that just underlined [the fact] that people who get on to a cricket field — it should be a sports field, but I only talk about a cricket field — should play the game hard and fairly and with good humour and do things that make it for the future a better game. I think that's what Worrell did.

2

IT'S A... IT'S A... IT'S A... TIE!

First Test

Brisbane: 9,10,12,13,14 December

Inevitably, the game's historians and commentators focus attention on Wes Hall's final over. After all, it is arguably the most fantastic over bowled in Test cricket. It should not, however, obscure the deeds of other redoubtable players who aided Hall in taking this match to rarefied heights quickening the pulse of a nation.

The fact that such a glorious celebration of the game was so unexpected heightened the impact of the occasion and ensured its precious niche in sporting history.

While there is reason to believe Frank Worrell happily engaged in an occasional innocent ruse to try and confuse Richie Benaud and the Australian selectors, the West Indies reached Brisbane in good spirits but with a very modest record. Certainly the more impatient critics expressed reservations about the calibre of the tourists and unhesitatingly made mention of the unfulfilled ambitions of John Goddard's team nine years earlier.

Garfield Sobers raises his arms in appeal and Rohan Kanhai jumps for joy as Joe Solomon's throw breaks the stumps with Ian Meckiff well short of his ground. Lindsay Kline looks back ruefully as redoubtable Frank Worrell surveys an unforgettable scene. *Ron Lovitt/Age*

41

A rare lapse in judgment from Alan Davidson as he survives Frank Worrell's emphatic leg before wicket appeal. Davidson became the first Test cricketer to aggregate 100 runs and take 10 wickets in a match.
News Ltd

The West Indies' only first-class success had come against Victoria after Rohan Kanhai gave notice of what lay ahead with a breathtaking double century. They were defeated by Western Australia by 94 runs and by New South Wales by a whopping innings and 119 runs. Draws against an Australian XI, South Australia and Queensland hardly enthused their supporters and a speedy innings victory over a West Australian country XI at Bunbury was of no consequence in the greater scheme of things.

While Benaud quietly prayed his damaged right index finger could withstand the rigours of a Test match, Alan Davidson confided to him that he too had damaged a finger and was uncertain whether he could take his injury into the match. Davidson, who had a reputation for exaggerating the extent of his aches and pains, agreed with Benaud that nothing was to be gained by alarming Sir Donald Bradman and his fellow selectors. He resolved to grin and bear any discomfort.

Worrell surprised the Australian team and the pundits in the press and broadcasting boxes by leaving Chester Watson out of the XI and taking it upon himself to open the bowling with Hall. There was no doubting his skills as an opening bowler, but at the age of 36 it was thought he had lost the venomous edge Watson could provide. Watson, however, had managed only eight wickets in four first-class lead-up matches. Furthermore, the West Indies' match with Queensland at the same ground the previous week had been dominated by the exploits of slow bowlers. Be that as it may, there was a perception that even a man of Hall's character, courage and stamina would be unfairly burdened.

The exhilarating tone of the match – and, indeed, the series – was established in the first session. Having won the toss, the West Indies refused to permit the early loss of Smith, Hunte and Kanhai to a rampant Davidson to disrupt their plans, and observers were left gasping at a lunchtime scoreboard of 3–130 with Sobers on 65 and Worrell 16.

Sobers, who at the age of 24 comfortably wore the mantle of the world's foremost batsman, had had, by his lofty standards, a modest preparation. His only substantial scores, of 119 and 72, had come in the second innings of matches against Western Australia and an Australian XI in Perth more than a month earlier. To add to his unease following a double failure against New South Wales in Sydney, there was speculation in the media that he could not pick Benaud.

Noticing Sobers was downcast, Sir Donald Bradman assured him he would get the runs when they were most required. Sir Donald had long been renowned for such perspicacity.

As though to demonstrate the extent of his indignation, Sobers mauled Benaud as he reached his century in 125 minutes. Finally he was out to a full toss from Meckiff for 132 (in 174 minutes with 21 boundaries), which took his aggregate of runs to 3054 in just 33 Test matches.

Commentators and writers rejoiced in the power and beauty of Sobers' innings, with A. G. 'Johnnie' Moyes saying Sobers had revived memories of halcyon days when Bradman and Stan McCabe were in their prime.

Sir Donald later described the innings as one of the finest he had witnessed.

Invariably, after a long partnership is broken the other party

Garfield Sobers was at the crease for just 174 minutes for his priceless 132 which commentator 'Johnnie' Moyes said revived memories of the batting of Sir Donald Bradman and Stan McCabe.
News Ltd

suddenly is out of kilter and vulnerable. Having added 174 in 152 minutes with Sobers for the fourth wicket, Worrell fell for 65 just four runs later. He had played with characteristic poise, struck eight fours in his 159–minute stay and, sensibly, happily provided the scintillating Sobers with the strike whenever possible.

Between them Sobers and Worrell had made a powerful statement about the intention of the third West Indies team to visit Australia.

If Benaud and Davidson believed the breaking of the partnership would see some normality return to proceedings, they were sorely mistaken. While history remembers Joe Solomon for two of the most accurate and telling throws ever made, he was also an accomplished batsman, and he made a well-crafted 65 before stepping on his wicket while endeavouring to swing Simpson to fine leg.

The cricket community was abuzz at the end of the first day, a day which had produced 359 runs, including 48 boundaries and one six. Inevitably, scribes made reference to the fact that two years earlier, England, in one hour less, had managed only 142.

And still the West Indies had more in store. Early on the second morning the flamboyant Hall joined Alexander at the crease. Gently rebuked by Sir Donald Bradman in the rooms the previous evening for failing to believe he could make a significant contribution with the bat, Hall engaged the Saturday crowd with an adventurous and often comical half-century with eight boundaries. With the more orthodox but no less powerful Alexander he added 86 runs in 69 minutes for the ninth wicket, and in the end the West Indies amassed an imposing 453 in better than even time.

Buoyed by his unexpected success as a batsman, Hall opened the bowling at a fearsome pace, and twice hit McDonald in the rib cage. The second blow was so severe McDonald's breathing seemed to be affected and his rib region was strapped during a drinks break. A month earlier McDonald, the grittiest of batsmen, had been badly battered by Hall while gathering a particularly plucky century for an Australian XI in Perth.

By the time he made his painful withdrawal with 57 after 111 minutes he had helped Simpson lay the foundation for the challenging pursuit.

The West Indians were already familiar with Simpson's wares, having seen him amass 87 and an undefeated 221 for Western Australia.

That he took four hours and 10 minutes over his 92 — 45 coming in singles — earned him some criticism from scribes who made a point of comparing Australia's run-rate with the West Indies'. At stumps on the second day Australia were 3–196 in 265 minutes.

After a restful Sabbath, O'Neill and Favell were poised to intensify the chase on Monday morning.

Like Simpson, O'Neill had wasted no time in strutting his stuff before the visitors. A fortnight earlier the 23-year-old had again dis-

While he will always be remembered for his thrilling run outs of Alan Davidson and Ian Meckiff, Joe Solomon made a substantial contribution as a middle-order batsman with scores of 65 and 47. Here he miscues a hook against Ian Meckiff.
News Ltd

regarded the pressure of being anointed the 'new Bradman', and composed a glorious undefeated 156 to provide New South Wales with an embarrassingly easy innings victory.

Initially, however, he could not recapture that same touch. He was unsettled after taking two hits on the body from Hall, and gave chances to Sobers off Worrell on 47 and to Alexander off Valentine seven runs later. The West Indies paid dearly for these lapses in concentration and judgment.

Aided first by Favell and then Mackay and Davidson, O'Neill gained in confidence as his innings blossomed. While his first 50 took 148 minutes his second came in 89 minutes with nine boundaries and his third in 90 minutes. By the time he gave Australia the first innings advantage he was again close to his irresistible best and was given a rapturous reception for his 181. He batted for six hours and 41 minutes, struck 22 boundaries and advanced his aggregate of runs beyond 1000 in his 14th Test. Remarkably, it was to be the only century by an Australian for the series.

That in the end Australia's advantage was not greater than 52 was due to the indefatigable Hall who bowled with greater control with the new ball and finished with four of the last five wickets.

The gloom that brought a premature close to proceedings on the third day lifted on cue and Hunte and Kanhai erased the deficit at breakneck speed — their 50 partnership for the second wicket coming in just 28 minutes.

Initially, not even the use of a deep third man and a deep fine leg threatened their ascendancy and Benaud summoned Mackay to help retard their progress. It proved a master stroke with Hunte chasing an outswinger he could have ignored and Mackay had his one wicket for the match. His job done, Mackay made way for Davidson who promptly yorked Sobers for 14 thereby precipitating a gleeful dance and returning the match to Australia's favour.

Had Worrell not been reprieved when Grout lunged in front of Simpson at slip Australia would have been in an even stronger position. It was a costly misjudgment as Worrell, with the support of Kanhai and the reliable Solomon, pushed the total beyond 200. With Solomon he added 83 for the fifth wicket before falling at 65 for the second time in the match. This time he occupied the crease for 151 minutes and struck nine fours.

With Meckiff worried by a tendon injury and unable to bowl, McDonald still suffering from the battering he took from Hall and Kline unwell, Benaud had to jolly his troops and give Mackay the new ball to share with the indomitable Davidson.

Occupation of the crease suddenly was as important as every run eked out. At one point Solomon and Alexander managed just 12 runs from 12 overs. Alexander held on grimly for 67 minutes until Benaud claimed his solitary wicket for the match and Solomon's admirable resistance finally ended after 222 minutes.

Given what occurred at the end of the day it is hardly surprising that events six hours earlier are rarely mentioned in despatches. But their significance should not be understated.

Hall and Valentine somehow contrived to stay at the wicket for a further 38 minutes and add another precious 25 runs. So by the time Davidson bowled Hall for 18 to finish with the imposing figures of 6–87 and lift to 11 his aggregate of wickets for the match, the 10th wicket stand was worth 31 and the West Indies total had reached 284.

For victory Australia needed to

Les Favell had no sooner struck Alf Valentine for successive straight sixes than he was run out for 45 after a mix-up with Norm O'Neill, Australia's only century scorer for the series. Alf Valentine looks on as keeper Gerry Alexander appeals. *News Ltd*

Frank Worrell, described by Sir Donald Bradman as a 'great cricketer in the artistic mould', executes a glorious cover drive against Alan Davidson. Non-striker Garfield Sobers, Bob Simpson and keeper Wally Grout look on admiringly.
News Ltd

score 233 runs at a rate of about 45 an hour. Benaud was convinced the target was attainable. So were his men.

Worrell had other ideas. So did his men — Hall in particular.

While it had taken him time to find his rhythm and control in the first innings, Hall exploded into action dismissing Simpson, Harvey, O'Neill and Favell in quick succession. With Worrell having accounted for McDonald half the side was gone for 57 and left-handers Mackay and Davidson were left to perform a miracle. Davidson, whose heroics with the ball had provided Australia with a priceless chance of victory now, had to focus on avoiding defeat. He could scarcely comprehend the speed with which Hall had transformed the game.

And when Ramadhin accounted for Mackay and Australia

sagged to 6–92 Australia's cause seemed hopeless. But Benaud, an eternal optimist, had other ideas.

At the tea adjournment Australia were 6–109 needing 124 runs in 120 minutes for an improbable victory.

As was his habit, Sir Donald Bradman made his way to the rooms for a cup of tea.

Looking straight at Benaud, Sir Donald asked: 'What's it going to be?

'Well, we're going for a win,' said Benaud.

'I'm very pleased to hear it,' replied Sir Donald.

While they had looked comfortable before the tea adjournment they were in command after it and with a mix of bold stroke play and daring running between wickets they added 134 for the seventh wicket in about even time.

With a remarkable victory within grasp Benaud counselled Davidson against taking any unnecessary risks running between wickets and then promptly committed him to an impossible single.

Rather than rejoice in the fact he had become the first man to aggregate 100 runs and take 10 or more wickets in a Test match, Davidson made a forlorn figure as he returned to the pavilion.

'Johnnie' Moyes described Davidson as 'shaking his head sorrowfully like the young man in the Parable.'

Grout, who had been chain-smoking in the pavilion, rushed nervously to the wicket, and to the penultimate ball of Sobers' last over picked up a single to leave Australia with six runs to score from the last over of the match. As hard as he tried Benaud couldn't get the final ball away to take strike to Hall's last over. That daunting task fell to Grout. Hall began to move in at 5.56.

THE LAST OVER

FIRST DELIVERY

The ball struck Grout an agonising blow in the solar plexus and then fell at his feet. The ball had barely hit the ground when Benaud called for a daring sundry which Grout completed in considerable discomfort.

SECOND DELIVERY

Despite a strict instruction from Worrell not to bowl a bumper Hall bowled a bumper. Benaud's eyes lit up as he saw the possibility of scoring four of the five runs that were required. His attempt to hook, however, failed and Alexander caught him at the wicket off his glove for a sterling 52. 'All yours, Wal ...' said Benaud as he headed for the pavilion. 'Thanks very much,' came the muttered reply.

THIRD DELIVERY

Meckiff played uneventfully to mid-off.

FOURTH DELIVERY

 Meckiff endeavoured to heave to leg but failed to make contact. As Alexander gathered down the leg side Grout called for the boldest of byes. Alexander under-armed the ball to Hall and Meckiff's run-out seemed inevitable. But rather than race Meckiff to the wicket or break the wicket with an underarm throw, Hall, despite being off balance, hurled the ball. He missed the wicket by some distance and Valentine reacted quickly at mid-off to save overthrows — quite probably four of them.

FIFTH DELIVERY

The fourth ball of perhaps the most fantastic over ever bowled. A wild throw from Wes Hall reprieves Ian Meckiff who scrambled a bye at the command of audacious Wally Grout. *Ron Lovitt/Age*

Grout sensed he was to receive a bouncer and moved into position to hook. But the ball was of a good length and he managed only to shovel it high to square leg. Kanhai, fielding behind square, ran forward to take a straightforward catch when Hall, who had abruptly changed direction, suddenly ran across him and dropped the catch. Furthermore, the ball ran some yards away from Hall and he had to quickly retrieve it.

Umpire Colin Hoy whose raised finger signalled the first tie in a Test match. *ABC*

SIXTH DELIVERY

Meckiff swung lustily and the ball headed for the mid-wicket boundary. Had early morning rain not disrupted the curator's preparations and cost him the time to cut the grass and clover flowers, the ball may well have reached the fence. Instead, Hunte fielded surely and turned and threw in one action. His throw on the bounce was flat, fast and accurate when Alexander lunged to remove the bails Grout was a foot short of his ground. Benaud wrote later that: 'Of all the minor miracles that took place on this day I give pride of place to this one.'

SEVENTH DELIVERY

With the scores tied and two deliveries remaining, Kline tremulously waited for Hall. The ball was in line with middle and leg and Kline played it towards square leg. Solomon, renowned as much for his dependability as his supreme skills as a fieldsman, moved swiftly to make a clean interception and with just one stump to aim at threw down the wicket. Umpire Colin Hoy's raised finger triggered scenes of high emotion on the players' veranda and among the crowd of 4100.

Many in the crowd jumped the fence and ran towards the exhausted players many of whom were uncertain of the result. Meckiff was distressed believing Australia had lost and Kanhai ecstatic at what he thought was an improbable West Indian victory.

It was some time before all the protagonists realised they had created history.

ON REFLECTION

ALAN DAVIDSON: To be quite honest, I was dirty.

JOE SOLOMON: As boys from the country we would pitch marbles and try to steal mangoes by hitting them down; we had a good aim.

RICHIE BENAUD
When you think that the captain with victory in sight has run out the guy who is just about to win the game — that was particularly stupid.

CAMMIE SMITH: To look at the face of those who had to go in ... Lindsay Kline, he was pale, pale, pale.

ROHAN KANHAI: There was no doubt when Grout skied that ball whose catch it was. I was under it, waiting for it when from nowhere there was a black arm over my face.

CONRAD HUNTE: I sensed Meckiff was bound to have a go at Wes Hall. And at that pace, 90 mph with the second new ball, it's bound to fly. So I quietly dropped back — which you should never do on a cricket field; never move before a captain moves you. I knew my one chance of getting him on the third run was to throw to Gerry Alexander. I was conscious he was running one, running two and turning for the third. I knew he had 22 yards and I had 90 and therefore I could only beat him by the quickest, fastest and lowest throw I'd ever thrown. When I got to the ball just before it got to the boundary I turned and, baseball style, I threw the ball to bounce on the square, to give it extra pace, to Alexander.

WES HALL
My captain said, 'Winfield, don't bowl a bouncer.' I said 'Okay, sir, I won't bowl a bouncer.' But in those days my bowling a bouncer was conditional not on whether the captain told me to bowl one or not but on how I felt in my run-up. If I felt good that is what you would get.

GERRY ALEXANDER: It was not quite as easy as it looked. I had to move to my right in front of the stumps. If I'd waited behind the stumps I don't think we would have got the run out. I remember feeling afterwards thank God I hadn't missed the stumps, because I was quite agitated keeping my eye on the ball, holding it and then swivelling to reach back for the stumps.

ALAN DAVIDSON: It had been such an incredible game of cricket. And take Wes Hall in the second innings. He'd got on a new pair of boots from Hope Sweeney at the start of the game. In the first innings his socks used to slide down on the new leather on the inside and they actually rolled down and formed a ball under the ball of his foot and he ended up with a dirty big blister. By the time the second innings came around that blister had really puffed up and eventually he had it pierced by the physio. He went out for the last session on the last day with a great slice of Elastoplast which had been spread over the blister. And by this time he'd cut around the blister and cut the whole piece of flesh out. So it was bare flesh and this Elastoplast over the whole lot and he went out without socks and bowled that last session. And that to me is one of the most awe-inspiring things I've ever seen. Forget whether it was your own team mate or otherwise, but to me that was courage beyond anything I'd ever seen, because if you saw him rolling in to bowl that last over; the way he roared in, the pain must have been excruciating. Yet here was this bloke giving his all. That and Sobers' 132 are the two things that came out of that tied Test. They're unforgettable moments for me.

IAN MECKIFF: Really, all I said to Lindsay was: 'If you hit it, we run.'

WES HALL: My captain, Frank Worrell said: 'There is only one thing I have to tell you. The scores are even right now and you have this ball and another ball. Please remember, do not bowl a no-ball, because if you do you will never be able to land in Barbados again.' I planted my foot a good 18 inches behind the crease.

ROHAN KANHAI: The last over was so tense that if you weren't strong inside I don't think you would have survived.

WES HALL: Pandemonium broke out — it was a wild scene. Everybody was excited except Worrell. He was there as passive as ever, and his knees buckled. I believe it was all that energy in marshalling his forces; he realised he'd not lost the game and he just sank — not to the ground, but his knees did buckle as if he'd received a right hook from Tyson.

ROHAN KANHAI: I thought at the time we had won.

GARFIELD SOBERS: I remember Rohan saying, 'We've won, we've won!' And somebody else saying the Aussies had won. Then somebody came up with the bright idea that if both teams had won then it must be a tie.

ALF VALENTINE: When the game concluded I said we'd lost by a run.

WES HALL: We were not sure; we thought we'd won, if anything, because certainly it wasn't a draw. I remember Meckiff saying: 'Fancy losing like that.'

PETER LASHLEY: The only conclusion I came to was that we weren't beaten.

IAN MECKIFF: I had a figure in my mind of 233 to win. And we hadn't made 233 and I just thought, well, that's the end of it.

LANCE GIBBS: I didn't know.

COLIN McDONALD: I thought, a tie, that's great; that'll do.

RICHIE BENAUD: We knew in the dressingroom what it was. No one was in the slightest doubt in our side.

GERRY ALEXANDER: We remember running off the field and querying what really had happened. We hadn't won but we hadn't lost. That's it — the two things flashed. But there was no such thing as a tie.

WES HALL: It was not in our cricketing upbringing to have a tie.

LINDSAY KLINE: I was running for a win but Ian was running for a tie. I believed the scores were tied but I didn't discuss it with Ian because I thought he knew. But as it turned out he didn't know.

ROHAN KANHAI: It took Richie quite a while to calm me down in the dressingroom.

RICHIE BENAUD: Frank (Worrell) was absolutely knackered. No question about that. So was I, but for a different reason — that we'd not won a cricket match we should have won.

JACKIE HENDRIKS: I remember betting half a crown with the Don on the result. And afterwards I said: 'You see, Sir Donald, you didn't win that time.' And he said: 'But I was only wrong by one run.' You could never get the last word with him.

RICHIE BENAUD: I said to the Don at the end: 'That's ridiculous — three run-outs in that short space of time and we had it there for the taking.' He said: 'Don't worry about it. You'll find that this is the greatest thing that has ever happened to the game of cricket.' I said; 'Well it's not at the moment.'

ALAN DAVIDSON: We had these tables set up and you had a West Indian and an Australian and a West Indian and an Australian all the way round, all mixed up together. And the champagne came out. That to me was the culmination of it all. Everyone had been through something massive, something unique, the first tie in Test history.

IAN MECKIFF

It wasn't until I got to the dressingroom afterwards that I knew. I still had the pads on and I grabbed a drink. Colin McDonald said: 'Why are you looking so unhappy?' I said: 'We've been beaten.' And he said: 'No, it's a tie.'

Not for the first time, plucky Colin McDonald is struck on the body by a wicked lifting delivery from fearsome Wes Hall. *Courier Mail*

3

THE GENERALS

A journalist who moonlights as Australian cricket captain is bound to enjoy certain privileges when it comes to the assigning of the cricket story of the day. Certainly there was no question in the mind of Sydney *Sun* sports editor Con Simons who should cover the arrival of Frank Worrell at Kingsford Smith Airport, Sydney in October 1960.

After all, Richie Benaud, the 30-year-old scribe oscillating between police, court and sports reporting, had been advised of Worrell's imminent arrival by Alan Barnes, who was in his first year as secretary of both the NSW Cricket Association (a position he had held since 1947) and the then Australian Board of Control for International Cricket.

Benaud had been appointed Australian captain in 1958 and would be Worrell's opposite number for the 1960–61 summer. Furthermore, Benaud knew Worrell and had the utmost respect for him as a man and cricketer.

Along with Colin McDonald and George Thoms, Benaud had

Entertainers from different spheres. Touring Trinidadian-born pianist Winifred Atwell in conversation with Frank Worrell and Alf Valentine (right) outside the Grey Smith Stand during the final Test match at Melbourne. *Alf Batchelder*
Left: Salute. The generals drink to a vintage summer. *News Ltd*

The good oil. Richie Benaud interviews Frank Worrell for the Sydney *Sun* on the tarmac at Sydney Airport. *Fairfax*

made his Test debut against Worrell in the final match of the 1951–52 series at Sydney and their paths crossed again in 1955, when Australia visited the Caribbean for the first time and enjoyed an emphatic 3–0 series success.

❁ ❁ ❁

Benaud was grateful for the assignment, as it allowed him to be the first to welcome Worrell back to Australia. It also enabled him to momentarily forget his frustration at being sidelined with a broken finger. He had seriously damaged the index finger of his right hand attempting a return catch while playing in Rhodesia (now Zimbabwe) for a Cavaliers team assembled by Ron Roberts, an entrepreneurial English cricket journalist given to organising multiracial cricket tours.

So Benaud had no option but to hand over the reins of New South Wales to Ian Craig for the opening Sheffield Shield match of the season (against Queensland in Brisbane) and report for work at the *Sun* office in Broadway.

As it happened, Worrell was also out of kilter, apparently after an encounter with some shellfish, to which he was allergic. However, great generals are self-sustaining, not self-pitying, and their conversation-cum-interview was characteristically upbeat and optimistic.

Sydney Airport was a modest place in those days, and Benaud and Worrell chatted and posed for photographs on the apron outside the terminal buildings. As Worrell made his way towards the *Lockheed Electra* which was to take him to Perth for the first three matches of the tour, Benaud called out: 'I hope it's a great summer.'

Worrell stropped, propped and came back a few yards and said with the broadest of smiles: 'We'll have a lot of fun, anyway.'

As ever, he was true to his word.

○ ○ ○

While he was barely 30 and six years younger than Worrell, Benaud had already forged a reputation as an astute and worldly captain. Well read and possessing the inquiring mind of the journalist, he had quickly learned the need for an awareness of the game's politics and power plays, and had an appreciation of the game's significance in the wider society.

As a part of his preparation for Australia's first full tour to Pakistan and India in 1959–60, Benaud had written to Prime Minister Menzies and asked to be briefed by a senior adviser to Richard Casey, the Minister for External Affairs.

Benaud went to Canberra and met with Peter Heydon, an assistant secretary in the Department of External Affairs. Heydon had been the Australian High Commissioner to India when Benaud played there with Ian Johnson's Australian team after the disappointing Ashes tour of 1956. Following the meeting the department despatched a communiqué to the Australian High Commissions in New Delhi and the old Pakistan capital of Karachi, seeking support

Prime Minister and passionate cricket follower Bob Menzies with Frank Worrell at his Prime Minister's match with the West Indians in February 1961. Menzies was knighted in 1963 and Worrell in 1964.
Fairfax

Richie Benaud introduced a new practice regimen when he took over the captaincy. *ABC*

and understanding for Benaud's pioneering party.

While the West Indies did not fulfil expectations on their visit in 1951–52, the contests were not as lopsided as the scoreline suggests, and plans for a reciprocal visit were soon put in train.

They were encouraged by Sir Robert Menzies and his friend the Captain-General and Governor-in-Chief of Jamaica, Sir Hugh Foot. Sir Robert, a noted devotee of the game and an unabashed admirer of one of Benaud's greatest heroes and mentors, Keith Miller, also did what he could to encourage Australia's first tour to the Caribbean in 1955.

Benaud was acutely aware of the social implications of Worrell's appointment as captain. Worrell was only the second black man to lead the West Indies and the first to take a team outside the Caribbean. George Headley, who was tagged the 'Black Bradman' after his tour to Australia in 1930–31, led against England at Barbados in 1948, but he was then in the autumn of his career and susceptible to injury. He played only two more Tests before retiring in 1953, at the age of 44, with a Test average of 60.83.

Keen observation in the West Indies five years earlier gave Benaud an appreciation of the pressures to which Worrell would be subjected now that he had finally and belatedly won the captaincy. For as long as Benaud could remember, the leadership of the West Indies had been an issue.

Indeed, Benaud's debut Test is remembered primarily because West Indies captain John Goddard stood down 20 minutes before

the start of play, delegating responsibilities to his deputy, Jeffrey
Stollmeyer. Goddard had managed
just 156 runs at 26.00 from seven
hands in the first four Tests, and
while the team had won in
Adelaide, it had consistently under-
performed. Victory had certainly
been thrown away in the first Test
in Brisbane.

By the mid 1950s the captaincy
was a cause célèbre, as Frank
Worrell's reputation as a cricketer
and statesman grew around the
world and forces within and
beyond the boundary pressed for
change. The loudest call for
Worrell's appointment came from
one of his legion of friends and

Frank Worrell, one of Richie
Benaud's five greatest cricketers of
the 20th century. *ABC*

admirers — CLR James, the distinguished and influential
Trinidadian writer, historian, social analyst and passionate cricketer
lover. James railed against colonial West Indies and vigorously used
his pen to show the world that Worrell was discriminated against.

The 1955 Australian team watched incredulously as the West
Indies captaincy was apparently manipulated. Speculation that
Worrell was in line for the job after he had acted as deputy to
Stollmeyer during the previous home summer against England
came to nothing. Stollmeyer was reappointed, with Denis
Atkinson as his lieutenant. As it happened, Atkinson led in three
matches and Stollmeyer in two.

Much more troubling, however, was the decision to name
Atkinson as the captain of the West Indies team to visit New
Zealand a year hence. This time the vice-captain was to be Bruce
Pairaudeau, predominantly an opening batsman from British
Guiana (now Guyana) who had had little success after making a
century on debut against India at Port of Spain in January 1953.
And he was not one of the 19 players the West Indies selectors

called upon as the Australians carried all before them.

Benaud had no doubt who should have been in charge:

Frank should have been captain. There was an undercurrent that became a rip tide at one stage when Jeff Stollmeyer was injured and Denis Atkinson was made captain. To make Denis captain when Everton Weekes, Clyde Walcott and Worrell were in that side was ... an insult. Everton and Clyde would have made good captains, but Frank was the leader. I'm quite certain that Denis was embarrassed, and he had every right to be. And Jeff Stollmeyer said: "What am I going to say to Frank?".

The West Indies played 27 Tests over the next five years before Worrell was finally appointed captain and James could rest. At the height of his campaign James wrote:

More important than this: Australia wants him as captain. This is the authentic fact. When Australian critics talk of Trumper, Kippax and the half-dozen batsmen who have batted as if they were born to it, they include Worrell. As a man he made a tremendous impression in Australia. Thousands will come out on every ground to see an old friend leading the West Indies. In fact, I am able to say that if Worrell were captain and Constantine or George Headley manager or co-manager, the coming tour would be one of the greatest ever.

In his renowned treatise, *Beyond a Boundary*, first published in 1963, James observed:

Worrell was finally appointed and then, strange but not unusual, there was universal jubilation. All classes approved. It is often so. Even those who had been led astray to give silent support to the extremists seemed genuinely relieved that the whole mess was over and they could participate with their fellow men in the general rejoicing. HBG Austin was the natural captain of the West Indies as long as he chose to play. You took that for granted. But I don't believe that any cricket appointment in the West Indies was ever so universally and warmly approved as that of Frank Worrell as captain of our team to Australia.

The constant clamouring for Worrell placed an enormous strain upon his predecessor, the outstanding wicketkeeper-batsman

Franz Copeland Murray Alexander, known to the international cricket community as 'Gerry'.

Alexander, a Cambridge University blue in 1952 and 1953, made his Test debut against England at Headingley, Leeds in the last week of July 1957. Six months later he was appointed captain — in only his third Test, the first with Pakistan at Bridgetown, Barbados — and he remained at the helm for the next 18 Tests until Worrell's appointment.

Yet Worrell played under Alexander only four times — in the home series against England in 1959–60. His studies prevented him from appearing against Pakistan in the Caribbean in 1957–58 and from making the long visit to the subcontinent for five Tests with India and three with Pakistan in 1958–59.

The groundswell for Worrell's promotion reached its height when Alexander returned to the Caribbean after winning 3–0 in India but losing 2–1 in Pakistan. Alexander was in Trinidad on his way back to Jamaica when it was officially announced that he would retain the captaincy for the home series with England in nine months' time — a series for which Worrell was available.

Alexander, who as a teenager in the summer of 1947–48 had played under Worrell in an inter-colonial trial for Jamaica, believed the decision of the game's governors to be premature, but was powerless to do anything about it. But a year hence, after the West Indies had lost to England in a series which produced four draws and speculation was rife about the leadership for Australia, Alexander certainly made it widely known that he believed Worrell's time had come.

Being a pawn in such a protracted social and political exercise had wearied Alexander. Benaud remembers Alexander saying: 'I'm, Worrelled out. I can't stand this any more.'

Having reached his 30s and just graduated as a veterinary scientist, Alexander's instincts were to earn a living rather than tour Australia. In the end, however, a distinguished contemporary, Allan Rae, persuaded him to make his swansong as Worrell's deputy Down Under. A more imposing conclusion to a career is hard to imagine. Alexander received rave notices for his performances as a keeper-batsman and for his wholehearted support of Worrell on and off the ground.

I had always felt I was only a stand-in for Frank until his studies were completed at Manchester University. Who was I to have an altercation with Frank? I was tremendously delighted when he was finally appointed captain. I thought the great injustice of my appointment against Pakistan in 1957–58 was not primarily to Frank Worrell but to Clyde Walcott and Everton Weekes. When I was made captain Clyde and Everton came to me and said there was a fine set of youngsters who wished to play under me, because they would never let the public say that because Gerry Alexander was captain of the West Indies team they didn't wish to play. They also said: 'Let me tell you, at the end of the Pakistan tour we will retire.' And in fact they did.

If Worrell carried the weight of the world on his shoulders as Caribbean cricket's first black captain and ambassador at large, it was not evident. In a matter of weeks he demonstrated what the elite cricketers of the West Indies and Australia had known for more than a decade: Worrell was born to lead.

As with all distinguished captains he made it is his business to understand the psychological profile of the disparate group of cricketers in his charge. And while much is rightly made of his skills as a strategist and communicator, Wes Hall also remembered Worrell's shrewdness:

He was a very good man when it came to the reward system. For instance, on a very hot day in Melbourne he would tell me, 'Winfield, if you give me 25, 27 overs today when the team goes to Ballarat and Berri over the weekend you'll go to Sydney and stay in a suite.' He got his 27 overs no problem at all. You can do that when you're 23 years old. He knew how to motivate players. And he didn't have to say, 'if the manager agrees'. He would have had that arranged with the manager. He was, too, very strict with curfews — into our rooms by 11 o'clock. But, as compensation, there was a television in every room — the first time I'd seen that. In the other games he never said you had to be in by 11. But he said: 'If your fitness is not right, I'm not going to pick you.'

○ ○ ○

Frank Worrell leads his men on to the Melbourne Cricket Ground during the fifth Test. Behind him come his deputy Gerry Alexander, Peter Lashley, 12th man Chester Watson substituting for Alf Valentine and Lance Gibbs. *Alf Batchelder*

While Worrell's entitlement to the leadership was being vigorously debated throughout the Caribbean and by expatriate West Indian communities far beyond the archipelago, Benaud ascended to the Australian captaincy in extraordinary circumstances.

Although his glorious tour of South Africa in 1957–58 contrasted starkly with that of his 22-year-old captain Ian Craig, there was no question of a palace revolt. Indeed, Victorian captain Neil Harvey was Craig's deputy, with Benaud further down the pecking order.

Benaud's brilliance — 30 wickets at 21.93 and 329 runs at 54.83 with two centuries — earned Australia an emphatic 3–0 success in the five-Test series and gave rise to widespread optimism that the precious Ashes, lost to Len Hutton in England in 1953, could be recovered against Peter May's 1958–59 visitors.

There was widespread speculation about whether Craig could justify his place as a batsman, however, having managed just 103 runs at 14.71 in the five Tests. Harvey, too, had had an unhappy time, dislocating the little finger of his left hand on the eve of the first Test at Johannesburg. He also had some debilitating illness, and in the end could point to just 313 runs at 21.83 with a top score of 68 — a galling return for one of the world's foremost batsmen.

Harvey was also seriously distracted by his modest financial circumstances and his frustration that the game's governors believed a Test fee of 75 pounds with 10 pounds expenses was a fair retainer.

When it became public knowledge that Harvey was considering pursuing his cricket career overseas, in the hope of making a respectable living, a Sydney businessman offered him work and a training program in the glassware industry. So in August 1958, barely two months before May's team began their tour in Perth, Harvey transferred to Sydney and provided the already formidable NSW team with even greater steel. Having succeeded Ian Johnson as Victorian captain in 1956–57, Harvey scored 836 runs at 104.50 and finished second in the aggregates, even though he only batted on 10 occasions.

Meanwhile, Craig had been diagnosed with hepatitis, so the NSW selectors entrusted Benaud with the captaincy for the opening Sheffield Shield match of the season against Queensland at the Gabba in October. This was only the second time Benaud had led New South Wales in a full match — the first was against Victoria in January 1956. Victory only just eluded New South Wales, whose imposing first innings total of 500 was inspired by Harvey's brilliant 160 in his first appearance for his adopted state.

Craig returned to the fray, but in successive weeks scored home ducks against Western Australia and the Marylebone Cricket Club (MCC) — it was patently and painfully obvious to critics and spectators that his comeback had been ill-timed. He had been seriously weakened by illness, and had little option but to rest for the remainder of the season.

A week after scoring 149 for New South Wales against the MCC, Harvey led an Australian XI against the tourists at Sydney. As speculation over the national leadership reached fever pitch,

Harvey made 0 and 38 and May's men won for the third time in their build-up to the first Test. The following day Benaud was announced as Australia's 28th captain. The first Test with England at the Gabba from 5 December 1958 was only his third outing as a captain in first-class cricket.

By the time he prepared to match wits with his friend Worrell at the same ground two years and four days later, Benaud was being feted as one of the most astute, innovative and intuitive leaders in the game. With Harvey as his faithful lieutenant, Benaud had quickly established an enviable reputation, winning the three series he had contested: at home against England and abroad against India and Pakistan. Eight wins, one loss and four draws from 13 Tests was his formidable record.

There was no sign, however, that Worrell was intimidated, despite entering the first Test with a deflating record of one victory, two losses and three draws from an intense six-match preparation as the team travelled east.

While Benaud was considered tactically superior to Worrell both were true leaders of men blessed with warm personalities and exceptional communication skills.

Since federation in 1901 and the creation of the Board of Control four years later, Australian cricket has been characterised by intense interstate rivalries, which have sometimes been magnified by apparent horse-trading at boardroom and selection tables. But such differences and jealousies are mere trifles compared with the differences that historically have riven the sovereign nations comprising the West Indies.

At various times in history cricket has been a powerful unifying force in the Caribbean — but only when the West Indies team has been expertly led and successful. At other times it has been divisive.

Worrell's greatest challenge initially was to ensure that the team was united in thought and endeavour. Not long before his death in Sydney in December 1999, Conrad Hunte recalled:

Frank was remarkable. In Perth he got us together and said: 'Gentlemen, on previous tours I have noted we easily segregate into little cliques within the team. I want none of that on this tour. I want us to play as a team on the field and live as a family off the field.'

With the unconditional support of his manager, Gerry Gomez, and assistant manager, Max Marshall, Worrell fused seven Barbadians, five Jamaicans, three British Guianese and a Trinidadian into a crack West Indian team. Gomez, in particular, understood the need for a united front. A fine all-rounder whose first-class career spanned 20 years — 1937–57 — he was a key member of the fragmented group which failed to fulfil expectations in Australia in 1951–52.

Gerry Gomez who toured as a player in 1951-52 returned as a popular and highly-respected team manager in 1960-61. *ABC*
Left: Debonair Richie Benaud emerges from the dressingrooms in the Grey Smith stand at the Melbourne Cricket Ground. Ken 'Slasher' Mackay and Alan Davidson follow their leader.
Alf Batchelder

Within days of arriving in Perth and joining the majority of his men, who had sailed to Fremantle aboard the liner *Strathaird*, Worrell put in place a leadership structure. He created 'cell groups', as he termed them, and appointed Alexander (his deputy), Hunte and Valentine cell leaders. He expected the leaders to deal with any problems that arose within their groups and to report to him at regular intervals. If a problem was too difficult for a cell leader, Worrell took charge. Players were free to circumvent their cell leader on confidential or personal matters; Worrell's door was always open.

That Worrell was unquestionably, unchallengeably the appropriate choice as captain provided him with a powerful position in the mind of Garfield Sobers, his successor against Australia in 1965:

I think Frank was fortunate that when he took over the players were around a certain age and there were no challengers. You do have times when as many as five or six players feel they should be captain. And that causes a lot of animosity among the team. But nobody else other than Sir Frank could captain the team, so therefore he had 100 per cent control and attention from every player in that team. That made his job easier. When you have a captain like that, a captain who knew the game and a captain that should have been captain before, from all that was said, you feel you've got to support him. And

he knows that whatever he says is going to filter down through the team and everybody is going to put their best foot forward because there is no resentment in the team. And he did a fantastic job and everyone was behind him.

Wes Hall congratulates Richie Benaud on his appointment as an Officer of the Order of the British Empire in February 1961.
News Ltd

Worrell was intent on ensuring that the team was not only united in thought and deed, but also that it was capable of earning the respect, admiration, even friendship of the Australian people. Worrell saw his charges as statesmen for a Caribbean region that was in the throes of the development of political independence, and he exhorted them to make an indelible impression on the Australian people.

Not in his wildest dreams could he have imagined what was to unfold.

As one would expect of an astute leader recently immersed in the social sciences at Manchester University, Worrell had made a close study of the characteristics and intrinsic strengths and weaknesses of his cricketers.

Privately, he spoke openly about his belief that West Indian players generally were given to a state of nervous anxiety and high emotionalism, especially at tense times in matches. Because of this, he was unconvinced of the worth of team meetings, and so called them sparingly. Experience had taught him that players could become restless and agitated if a captain or manager held the floor too long expounding opinions and theories.

But when team meetings were called, every player was encouraged to participate. Furthermore, he ensured that each player understood exactly why a particular XI was chosen at a given time. He left no room for speculation that selection could be influenced by anything other than cricket.

Worrell's calm and confidence inspired and empowered his men. Certainly Alexander felt more powerful, more influential.

Frank enjoyed the full and absolute confidence of everyone in the side. If Frank said move to your right you simply asked how far to the right. No one had to be concerned too much about what was happening in the middle. Frank was in charge and no one had any doubts that whatever he was going to do was in the best interests of the team. Frank always had a reason. This was a remarkable support to feel on the field. He had his own knowledge of where a game was going and he was not afraid. He allowed things to flow.

Frank Worrell was renowned for his calm and conscientiousness both on and off the ground.
News Ltd

While Worrell had serious reservations about the merit of team meetings, Benaud enthusiastically embraced such forums. He was an innovator from the time he took office, initiating the vigorous training session on the eve of a match which is now part of every team's regimen and encouraging greater effusiveness from his men on the field — especially at the fall of a wicket.

While Worrell had been spared the tedium of Test cricket in the late 1950s as he studied at Manchester University, Benaud had been at the front line, and clearly understood the need to revitalise the game by playing attractive cricket.

Under Benaud Australia had regained the Ashes in 1958–59 by a handsome 4–0 margin, but it is not a series remembered for its celebration of the game. Indeed, even 40 years later, any mention of the series is invariably prefaced by derogatory observations about Trevor Bailey batting for seven hours and 38 minutes for 68 in the first Test at Brisbane.

A year later Peter May took England's funeral fare to the Caribbean. He alienated more watchers by using methods of attrition to win the series — with a solitary victory and four matches drawn. It was a wholly unsatisfactory exercise, and gave Gerry Alexander another reason to consider bringing forward his retirement:

Against the MCC we had six days of five hours' cricket. When you got up on the morning of the seventh day — we had a rest day — you wondered why you were there. But Frank didn't know anything of this negativism. He just wanted to go out and play. And he was matched by Richie. It was amazing. We would get up in the morning, and unlike previous Tests we couldn't wait for 10 o'clock. It was remarkable. It was hard to believe that with this sort of enthusiasm and feeling we were playing Test cricket.

Benaud knew from discussions with the chairman of selectors, Sir Donald Bradman, that concern for the general welfare of the game was felt deeply and widely. Sir Donald, who but for a short period in the 1950s had been involved in the selection of every Australian team since 1936–37, had become more aware of the disquiet within the cricket community since his appointment as chairman of the Australian Board. The first Test cricketer elected to the lofty office, Sir Donald succeeded Victorian Bill Dowling a matter of weeks before chairing the panel to name the team for the first Test with the West Indies in Brisbane.

The fact that Benaud had introduced team meetings when he took over the captaincy two years earlier had not escaped Sir Donald's attention. These were simple, unsophisticated gatherings around a convivial ale where Benaud could turn to his deputy Harvey and to Colin McDonald and Wally Grout for support.

Given that Sir Donald fervently believed the series against the West Indies could reinvigorate Test cricket throughout Australia and beyond, he asked Benaud if he could speak at the team meeting on the eve of the first Test.

After first getting the blessing of his players, Benaud welcomed Sir Donald to the team meeting at Lennons Hotel in Brisbane, and to a man the Australians listened intently as the most influential voice in world cricket spoke of Test cricket and its future. And he left them in no doubt that the selectors would look kindly upon those who played attractive, enterprising cricket during the season.

For cricket's sake, there was a need to entertain, he said.

Six days later the first Test match was tied — Sir Donald could scarcely contain his excitement as he congratulated Benaud and Worrell on overseeing the greatest match since Test cricket began in March 1877.

Just 6 years and 3 months later, Worrell died of leukemia. He was 42. He is buried on high ground at the Barbados campus of the University of the West Indies at Cave Hill, a few minutes' drive north of his native Bridgetown.

At the time of the Australian visit to the Caribbean in 1995, Benaud proudly delivered the annual Sir Frank Worrell Memorial Lecture at the University:

Frank was one of the great people. He might not get into the list of great captains from a purely tactical point of view, but just think for a moment at being the first black man to captain the West Indies overseas. And the things he did and the way he did them. That was even more to the point. I don't know that you'd find anyone in the world who had a harsh word to say about Worrell. He was a great guy. I spent a bit of time on what I was going to say and thoroughly enjoyed saying it. It was nice to be able to pay a tribute to a great person. It was very moving for me.

Significantly, Benaud included Worrell in his five players of the 20th century in the poll conducted by *Wisden Cricketers' Almanack* for its 137th (and millennium) edition.

ON WORRELL

NEIL HARVEY: The best thing the West Indies did was to make Frank Worrell captain. He did a Richie Benaud. He just bolted these guys together. You wouldn't get a nicer guy than Frank. He was a real gentleman and he got on very well with Richie and the rest of the Australian players. And we got on very well with him.

CONRAD HUNTE: Frank was like a father to us, so when he became the first black captain we were rejoicing because we knew something special was going to happen. Frank had been first vice-captain and then captain of Commonwealth teams in India (deputising for Les Ames in 1950–51) and then a graduate of Manchester University. So we knew he brought to the table something more than his colour, and that's exactly what happened. He was the perfect choice as captain.

GARFIELD SOBERS: He was a great leader; a great student of the game. He never seemed to wilt under pressure. He was always so relaxed and so calm. You couldn't believe that even when things around you seemed so far away from you that a man could be so calm and collected and keep the team that way. I think this is one of the reasons it was such a great tour. I don't think anybody really got flustered or there was any real tension because the captain was always so cool, so calm and collected. The things he did quietened you down and kept you in a similar fashion.

ALAN DAVIDSON: You can't be a hero unless you've earned it, and Frank was one of the three Ws. When Worrell took over he had that father image, but at the same time he was also a hero in the eyes of every one of his players. I would have said that by the end of that series he was an even bigger hero, because he was a hero in our eyes as well. He moulded them from a team of brilliant individuals into a pretty useful team by the time the series was over.

ALF VALENTINE: You could talk to Frank. He was a good listener who liked people and had a lot of time for them socially. He had a way of getting to you and getting the best out of you. That he was our first black captain did a lot for the guys. They played their hearts out for him.

GERRY ALEXANDER: The great thing about Frank was that he was approachable. He was an easy-going, almost soft person. He enjoyed the full and absolute confidence of everyone.

WES HALL: Sir Frank was a great motivator. He wasn't filling everyone's motivational tank every ball, but he certainly was quietly letting you know who you were and his expectations of you. He was the first captain that I ever played with that really understood what management was about. He would manage players individually and as a team. He was a strategist and a great communicator. He had the utmost confidence of the team. To me as a very young man he seemed to understand that leadership itself was an art. Sir Frank would say things in the middle of an over which would inspire you. He would tell you what he wanted and you would be scolded if you disobeyed. But in the end, you know, I loved him for it, because you needed someone, a father figure, who would tell you what to do. I've never known a greater man.

BOB SIMPSON: Frank didn't show a great deal of flamboyance on the ground. He was very quiet in his control. I think the genius of Frank Worrell lay in what he did off the field. He got that team together as the West Indies, not a bunch of individuals representing different countries from the West Indies. I think this was his great skill. He wasn't a particularly aggressive captain. We felt he was pretty negative as far as bowling was concerned. He concentrated on wearing us down a fair bit. But he certainly had the respect of everyone, including the Australian team.

ON BENAUD

ALAN DAVIDSON: He was an incredible player. I can honestly say he is the most intelligent cricketer I have played with or against.

He had an incredible cricket brain — his analysis of a moment in time on a cricket ground; sensing when something was going to happen; his movement of a fieldsman. Wally Grout used to say he could dip his head into a bucket and come up with a mouthful of diamonds. I suppose to a point you've got to be lucky, but at the same time his judgment of his own players' capabilities and the opposition was just uncanny. He set the example so well, and I think that's captaincy at the highest level.

BOB SIMPSON: Richie was a man of enormous confidence. He was an actor. He was a great actor. Everything he did was arranged and planned. He was very precise, and I think gave you a great deal of confidence and calm. He always seemed on top of things. He never got flustered about it and I think that was the strength of his captaincy. He had a very, very good team to captain as far as attitudes to the game. I think he was the perfect person to take advantage of the situation. In New South Wales we were used to setting the pace, and we appreciated there was a problem with cricket and if we could get 350–400 we just closed overnight. That was it. Then we backed ourselves to bowl the opposition out. Some exciting times then.

NEIL HARVEY: Richie was a very good captain. We're good mates and toured together to the West Indies as room-mates in 1955 and England in 1956. He was the first, to my knowledge, to have team meetings. I think this is the guy who probably instilled more team spirit than had ever been done before. I know it's been done since, but this was the start of it all.

IAN MECKIFF: Richie was a professional, I suppose, in an amateur world. We were amateurs in those days, in comparison to what it is today. But by the same token Richie was very professional in everything he did. Everything had to be spot on; his preparation, the way he went about it. Everything. There's no doubt that was one of Richie's strong points.

4

VILLAINOUS SKIPPER BENAUD

Second Test

Melbourne: 30,31 December, 2,3, January

The Test that followed the tied match was destined to be an anticlimax. It was just not possible for the protagonists to play with the same manic intensity that had captivated the cricket world — it had left them physically, mentally and emotionally spent.

And so, after the heady heights of Brisbane, the West Indies suffered the ignominy of following-on, and lost by seven wickets. Nevertheless, the match occupies a special place in the annals of cricket and is often recalled because of a curious incident that instantly became a part of the lore of the game.

Joe Solomon, promoted to open the innings in place of Cammie Smith, was correctly given out 'hit wicket' after his cap fell from his head and dislodged the off bail as he played back to Richie Benaud.

Richie Benaud at 70 and the game's pre-eminent critic and commentator. *Scott Barbour/Allsport*

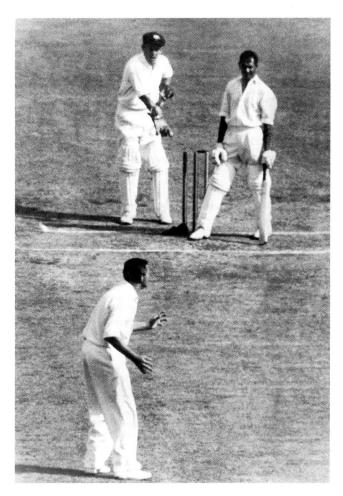

The incident that caused the third-day crowd of 65,372 to boo Richie Benaud to the echo. Joe Solomon is bowled when his cap falls and dislodges the off bail while playing back to Benaud. Keeper Wally Grout makes certain all and sundry know exactly who is at fault.
News Ltd

Nearly 40 years later Solomon is still disbelieving. 'My cap fell on the wicket — and this is a slow bowler not a fast bowler; I'm not ducking a bouncer. A slow bowler, play back, my cap fell off, hit the stumps,' he says forlornly.

For the second time in as many Tests unassuming Solomon's name was in headline type in newspapers throughout the land.

As Wally Grout pointed to the bail on the ground umpire Colin Hoy upheld the appeal, much to the dismay and annoyance of many in the third-day crowd of 65,372. Disenchanted supporters loudly jeered Benaud — they believed he had acted in an unsportsmanlike manner and should have recalled Solomon. The fact Benaud had stuck strictly and fairly to the laws of the game did little to mollify them.

The crowd reaction stunned the critics, but it illustrated the extent of public support the West Indies had garnered following their gallant showing in Brisbane. Certainly it offended the sensibilities of the noted broadcaster and writer 'Johnnie' Moyes. He wrote: 'Whenever he [Benaud] started to bowl the yelling would continue and not for some time did the unruly mob cease its turbulence. It was a nasty scene and most discreditable.'

Benaud was accustomed to bouquets, not brickbats, and had followed his inspirational performance at the Gabba by leading New South Wales to their second innings victory over the tourists and with a day to spare.

Given that Melbourne was sweltering in temperatures of over 100°F (38°C), winning the toss gave Benaud the chance to intensify the pressure by batting first. The West Indian bowlers, including Chester Watson on this occasion, soon learned that there is no respite from the heat in the middle of the MCG on a still day.

Nevertheless, they went about their work uncomplainingly, and had the satisfaction of removing Colin McDonald, Neil Harvey and Bob Simpson by lunch. Had it not been for Solomon, at fine leg slip, putting down a difficult chance offered by Norm O'Neill — on two — off Garfield Sobers, the session would have been even more productive.

While O'Neill, Les Favell, Ken Mackay and Alan Davidson contributed cameo hands of varying competence, only Mackay bettered 70, and the persistence of the West Indians looked to be handsomely rewarded, with Australia 8–251 soon after tea.

In Johnny Martin, Mackay found a resourceful and bold ally against the sweat-streaked and jaded bowlers late in the day. They rapidly added a telling 97 for the ninth wicket, with Martin, in his first Test innings, reaching his half-century in just 79 minutes.

Solomon, promoted to open following Smith's omission, ambitiously attempted to cut the seventh ball of the West Indies' first innings against Davidson, but succeeded only in providing a catch to Grout. His dismissal signalled stumps on the first day.

The second day began bleakly for the West Indies, with Conrad Hunte edging the third ball of the morning to Simpson at slip to give Frank Misson his first Test wicket.

Rohan Kanhai, however, was unperturbed by the seriousness of the predicament and played with characteristic daring from the start. Conversely, Seymour Nurse, who had been preferred to Peter Lashley, struggled to find touch and was lucky to be reprieved early by Harvey. He survived to lunch, however, by which time some order had been restored; the West Indies were 2–105, with the irrepressible Kanhai on 69. The second fifty of their unbroken stand of 104 took just 35 minutes.

But Melbourne's famously fickle weather put paid to the West Indies' hopes of continuing the revival, and only another 22 minutes of play was possible. Kanhai was compelled to play with great care to survive against Benaud in the fading light.

The vast holiday Monday crowd came in anticipation of another batting celebration of the kind that had set the series alight in Brisbane. Instead, they saw a capitulation.

While Nurse battled manfully to finally reach 70, the loss of the ebullient Kanhai for 84 precipitated an extraordinary collapse — the last eight wickets falling for 57 runs. Indeed, no one other than Kanhai and Nurse reached double figures, and the loudest applause came for Davidson, who took 5–29 to finish with the figures of 6–53, and Benaud, who conceded just 25 runs from 16 overs and, to boot, claimed the precious wicket of Sobers.

Mindful of a forecast for more unsettled weather, Benaud had no hesitation in asking the West Indies to bat again, despite his concern that Davidson and Mackay were both sore and receiving treatment. Apparently oblivious to the hubbub caused by his refusal to recall the luckless Solomon, Benaud planned his attack with characteristic precision, and at stumps the West Indies were in desperate straits at 5–129 — still requiring 68 to avoid an innings defeat.

While Solomon received a consoling word or two from fieldsmen close to the bat, there was no question in the mind of those familiar with the laws that he was out. His habit of batting so far inside the popping crease left him in considerable danger — and, indeed, contributed to his dismissal in Brisbane when he stood on his wicket while sweeping Simpson.

Following the smart run-out of Nurse by Davidson, Martin caused a sensation by taking his first three wickets in Test cricket in just four deliveries. And what prizes they were: Kanhai miscuing to Misson, and then, in his next over, Sobers and Frank Worrell caught by Simpson at slip — Worrell completing a dreaded pair.

It was a magnificent moment for Martin. He had accounted for Worrell for 28 and 0 the previous week when playing for New South Wales, thus advancing his claim for inclusion in the XI, and had now completely justified that inclusion.

The weather was bleak and threatening again on the fourth day, and a shower drove the players from the field before a ball was bowled. But while it remained cool and overcast, there were no fur-

Keeper Gerry Alexander takes a glorious diving catch to dismiss Neil Harvey for a duck in the second innings. Harvey knows his fate and sees no reason to look back.
Sydney Morning Herald

ther interruptions as Hunte and the reliable Gerry Alexander attempted to extricate the West Indies from the mire.

Hunte, renowned for his willingness to sacrifice flair and daring for the sake of team endeavour, moved beyond a most deserved century before he got the faintest nick to a full toss from O'Neill. He had batted for 270 minutes, struck nine boundaries, and added 87 with Alexander. Yet another of Benaud's variations on a theme had paid an immediate dividend.

With Hunte's dismissal Alexander had to go it alone. He showed enormous character, and returned his highest Test score — 72 (in 194 minutes, with seven boundaries) — but for all his gallantry, in the end Australia needed just 67 runs to take a precious lead in the series.

With customary flamboyance, Wes Hall told manager Gerry Gomez to keep a close eye on him if he wanted to see truly fast bowling. Hall was as good as his word and generated frightening speed: Australia lost McDonald, Harvey and O'Neill before fearless Favell steered them to victory by seven wickets.

At a press interview Worrell defended the right of Hall and Watson to bowl bouncers, pointing out as diplomatically as possible that he considered a number of the top-order Australians vulnerable against deliveries above hip height.

ON REFLECTION

GARFIELD SOBERS: We knew he [Solomon] was out. There was no hesitation in the West Indies camp by the West Indies players, because it is a part of the rules of cricket.

RICHIE BENAUD: There were 70,103 people there, I think. And there would have been at least 11 or 12 who didn't boo me that day.

CONRAD HUNTE: It really was quite interesting. I remember the crowd booing Richie Benaud for some time — which is quite unusual.

GARFIELD SOBERS: The games had gone so well and the relationship between the teams and the Australian people was such that they thought probably at the time that Richie and the team should not have appealed. But it's a part of the rules, and you have to appeal, otherwise you are not keeping within the laws of the game.

CONRAD HUNTE: I think it was a measure of how much the West Indians under Frank Worrell had begun to win the respect and admiration of the Australian crowds. And therefore, technically and legally Joe Solomon really was out, but they saw it, understandably, as not quite sportsmanlike.

NEIL HARVEY: I can understand the Melbourne public being a little bit upset about it because the West Indies team were so popular.

BOB SIMPSON: We felt the locals were supporting the Windies more than us on a few occasions because they'd been caught up in the whole thing. They loved the style of the West Indies and they had received really great publicity. So when that happened, we said 'Oh! He's out', and sort of started to gather around and a have a bit of a chat. Joey walked off and then suddenly the crowd was really booing Richie, which was totally unfair. It was a very tough call for him. There was no way he could recall the batsman; the man was out legitimately. So it was a clear-cut decision. But the crowd didn't like it. We didn't resent the crowd support they got, but you get a little jealous of it when you are used to local support and you're not getting it as much. But we accepted it as a compliment to the series, really. We could understand their emotions and also understand their relief that the West Indies were performing after a poor start and they were getting a great Test series.

CONRAD HUNTE: I think it was emotional. I think it was the fact that the Australians were beginning to be on our side and saw the way we played cricket. It was Sir Donald Bradman who said we put the 'C' back into cricket. And I think it was beginning to show, and that's why they began to support us against their captain Richie Benaud: a very remarkable thing.

PACEMAN, POLITICIAN, PREACHER

In the minds of many, Wesley Winfield Hall is the embodiment of the West Indian cricket person. He is imposing in stature, has a magnetic personality, is open and generous, laughs loudly and often and celebrates life as he celebrated cricket in his salad days: with gusto and daring.

A jovial man of character and charm, one is irresistibly drawn to him. He was the man long before IVA Richards was the man. In his early 60s now, he remains a charismatic soul with a remarkable capacity to reinvent himself.

At the age of 53 and at the height of a political career he became a Christian, and now, as an ordained minister in the Pentecostal Church, he preaches the gospel as well as his love of cricket and of his tiny, alluring homeland of Barbados.

'I thank God that he has allowed me to move from one profession to another,' says Hall. 'Whatever God asks me to do I will do. I didn't want to be a priest in the first place but if you have a calling you have to answer that calling.

'When you walk with God you walk with your faith. You have

Left: Charismatic Wes Hall.
Trent Parke

to let it show. It's not what you say, it's how people see you as a person.'

While he was raised in the Pentecostal Church by three women of god — his mother Iona, grandmother Louise and aunt Daphne — his initial calling was to his beloved game of cricket.

At St Giles primary school and Combermere secondary school he played his cricket as an opening batsman and wicket-keeper, and it was not until he approached his 19th birthday that he first pushed off his long run. By any measure his progress was extraordinary — barely eight weeks after his 21st birthday he came of age as a fast bowler, spearheading the West Indies attack on a demanding visit to India and Pakistan.

It said as much for Hall's temperament and courage as for

A formidable sight. Wes Hall begins to gather momentum ... *Right:* And eventually into his delivery stride. *ABC*

his abundant skills that he completed the tour with 46 wickets at 17.7 in five Tests against India and three against Pakistan. Furthermore, he returned match analyses of 11–126 in his second Test against India at Kanpur and 8–77 in his second Test against Pakistan at Dacca (now Dhaka, the capital of Bangladesh). In the final Test against Pakistan at Lahore he became the first West Indian to take a Test hat-trick, dismissing Mushtaq Mohammad — who was making his debut at the age of 15 and 124 days — captain Fazal Mahmood and Nasim-ul-Ghani. The West Indies won by an innings and 156 runs, thus inflicting the first home defeat on Pakistan since they entered the international arena in October 1952.

Despite communications with the Indian subcontinent and the Caribbean being unsophisticated, if not primitive, in the 1950s, news of Hall's awesome power and speed spread quickly on the cricketers' grapevine, with its nerve centre in the English leagues.

That he had followed his outstanding tour of India and Pakistan with 22 wickets at 30.86 in a tedious home series against a characteristically unimaginative England in 1959–60 was duly noted. Certainly particular interest was shown in his startling returns of 7–69 at Sabina Park, Kingston, Jamaica and 6–90 at the delightful Bourda ground at Georgetown in British Guiana (now Guyana).

Hall was a professional with the Accrington Cricket Club in the Lancashire League when he boarded the liner Strathaird at Southampton the week of his 23rd birthday for the voyage to Perth — via the Red Sea and Bombay — where he had made his Test debut two years before. The amateurs travelled by plane.

Given that the journey took six weeks, Hall had ample time to consider more than his immediate future as an elite cricketer. A politicised young man with a good grasp of cricket history, he had often wondered why 'Black Bradman' George Headley had not captained the West Indies throughout the 1930s. Clearly Headley had been the best West Indian cricketer of the period, and did not the best player generally captain the team? Why had Headley only once captained the West Indies, at the age of 38 and at the very end of his remarkable career?

Hall considered it a singular honour and great privilege to be chosen to play under Frank Worrell — the first black man to lead the West Indies outside the Caribbean. Worrell, too, was an old boy of Combermere School.

While he privately lamented the fact that the selectors had not chosen his friend and Barbadian team-mate Charlie Griffith, he was determined to have a good time on and off the field. This he accomplished without trouble, and with considerable flair.

News of Hall's fearsome pace spread like wildfire after his first appearance in Australia, in the match with an Australian XI in Perth the first week of November. Although he bowled erratically and was responsible for most of the 34 extras in the Australian innings of 194, he rejoiced in the hard, fast, bouncy and true deck on offer at the WACA ground. His abiding affection for Australia, Australians and Australian pitches and Australian racecourses had its genesis in Perth.

To watchers and critics, all brimful with expectation, it was patently clear that Hall would be a formidable, menacing opponent for the Australian batsmen.

Certainly Colin McDonald, Neil Harvey and Norm O'Neill, who were all considered certain to play in the Tests, returned to the eastern states with graphic tales of Hall's speed and venom. McDonald, who had opened the batting with Bob Simpson, took some fearful blows to the body. As it turned out, this was just the beginning of a torrid time for Australia's openers generally, and for McDonald in particular.

It was also immediately evident that Hall was one of the most distinctive personalities among the visitors. He made a wondrous sight in full stride on his slightly angled approach, the buttons of

Awesome. Wesley Winfield Hall in full cry. *ABC*

his white shirt unfastened and his signature gold crucifix bouncing and glistening against his black torso.

His enthusiasm was boundless, and many of his gestures and antics were comical; and he was soon embraced by crowds the length and breadth of the country. Since the days of the Demon Spofforth crowds have keenly identified with charismatic fast bowlers, and Hall demanded to be watched.

His special place in the history of the game was assured after he bowled the final over of the tied Test match in Brisbane — perhaps the most fantastic over ever bowled.

Furthermore, as one of international cricket's foremost humorists and raconteurs, his recounting of the over now occupies a special place in the rich lore of the game. It may not be the most accurate recollection, as he will attest, but it is captivating. Perhaps his greatest rendition of the magnificent seven deliveries came in 1979, when he shared a stage with the legendary British racing driver Stirling Moss at Dunedin, in New Zealand. Happily, this telling of one of cricket's most remarkable tales was recorded, and subsequently many thousands of the game's devotees around the world have been greatly entertained.

Wait, yes, no, sorry. Crowds everywhere thrilled to Wes Hall's antics as a batsman. But by no means was he inept at number 10 and for the series pointed to 158 runs at 17.55 with one of his two Test career 50s coming in the tied Test at Brisbane. ABC

'I confess I didn't know what I said and I was relying on the posturings of my subconscious as I told that story,' he confided during one of his frequent visits to Australia. 'And I must apologise for calling [Ian] Meckiff a monumental rabbit. "Mecko", I ask your forgiveness. Let's say he wasn't a Norm O'Neill. I think we can settle for that!'

Such was his fondness for Australia, he returned between international engagements to play for Queensland in 1961–62 and 1962–63 and the Randwick District Cricket Club in Sydney in 1966–67.

He returned again as a member of Garfield Sobers' touring party in 1968–69 but was at the end of his career, and made just two appearances, in the third and fifth Tests in Sydney. He went on to New Zealand and played his 48th and last Test match at Eden Park, Auckland the first week of March 1969.

'Wes was a magnificent bowler,' says Richie Benaud. 'He wasn't quite as quick as Frank Tyson, and Ray Lindwall was very fast. But Wes was right up there and just short of Tyson's pace. Not as quick as Jeff Thomson, but very quick. He had good control, [and] not so much a change of pace, although he did have a slower ball. But he did move the ball off the seam and he had a wonderful outswinger. He was right in the top bracket of all the pace bowlers that have ever been.

'And he was always a great character off the field as well. There was never a dull moment when Wes was batting or bowling or fielding. He was just that sort of player. A wonderful part of the scene in world cricket round about that time.'

While he made a comfortable transition from the sporting field to the political arena, he remained closely involved with the Caribbean cricket community, serving the West Indies as a team manager and selector. Indeed, it is among his proudest claims that not one of the many teams he managed during the 1980s lost a Test series. And he has the unique distinction of having played alongside or managed every West Indies captain from John Goddard (who led in 22 of his 27 Tests and was at the helm in Australia in 1951–52) to the incumbent Jimmy Adams.

He served the Barbados parliament for 23 years in both the

upper and lower houses, and at the height of his career was a member of the cabinet as the Minister for Sport and Tourism in the governments of Erskine Sandiford.

Hall has maintained some business interests in Barbados' buoyant tourist industry and has some government consultancies, but it is his unpaid ministry that occupies most of his energy. For three years he commuted to Miami, Florida to train for the priesthood and now he occasionally preaches at his church in the Barbados capital of Bridgetown, with his committed congregation of about 3000.

At the start of the new millennium his passionate interest was in a sports ministry and a prison ministry. He preached at the funeral of Malcolm Marshall in November 1999 and believes he led arguably the greatest of all fast bowlers to Christ shortly before his death.

Hall was reared by his mother and grandmother in a housing development in Bridgetown, and he proudly declares his membership of the proletariat. His love and admiration for the people is undiminished. And undiminished, too, is the love and respect of folk everywhere for this man of God, this cricketer of the people, this charismatic soul and wonderful storyteller.

The paceman and his admirers. At 23, Wes Hall, the signature gold crucifix around his neck, is an imposing figure as he makes his way on to the Melbourne Cricket Ground in February 1961.
Alf Batchelder

6

AUSTRALIA IN A SPIN

Third Test

Sydney: 13, 14, 16, 17, 18 January

t said much about Frank Worrell's capacity to captivate, counsel and cajole that the West Indies conquered their fears of the Sydney Cricket Ground to win handsomely and level the series.

Two earlier visits to the ground had proved disastrous, with innings defeats against New South Wales before and after the tied Test. While Worrell made it clear that the team's energies were being principally directed at the Test matches, the extent of the losses were, nevertheless, subduing.

These West Indian cricketers, like their many successors over the next 40 years, were deeply suspicious of the wicket block. In a forthright interview with the *Sydney Morning Herald*, Worrell declared that a pitch which turned so much on the first day and was uneven in bounce was not appropriate for Test cricket. Furthermore, he suggested

Garfield Sobers hits out against Richie Benaud during his thrilling innings of 168. In this instance he was on 48 and fortunate a miscued pull did not fall on his stumps. Keeper Wally Grout takes evasive action. *ABC*

that such conditions would have a deleterious affect on the quality of Australian batsmanship if prompt action were not taken.

Unlike the first two Tests, the West Indians went into the match on the back of victories — by 139 runs over a Combined XI at Hobart and by six wickets against Tasmania at Launceston. Their humour was further improved when Worrell won the toss and spared them the anguish of batting last. And to further lift their spirits, the sun shone strongly for one of the rare times in the match and the pitch was superior to those of earlier visits and held far fewer fears.

Nevertheless, they did not take advantage of the conditions in the first session as much as they had hoped to, losing Cammie Smith, Conrad Hunte and Rohan Kanhai for 94. At the same time, Alan Davidson, Ian Meckiff and Ken Mackay all moved the ball in the air and off the seam. Meckiff had recovered from injury and was reinstated at the expense of Frank Misson while Mackay also needed to be passed fit by doctors.

The disappointment of losing Hunte — when he had again promised so much — eased after the adjournment when Garfield Sobers showed signs of regaining the touch that had brought him such rave reviews at the start of the series.

Before lunch, he had been strangely uncertain — presumably the consequence of spending so little time in the middle since the tied Test. In the 30 days since the euphoria of Brisbane, Sobers had managed just 9 and 0 in the second Test, 2 and 18 against the Combined XI and 57 and 29 against Tasmania.

With Worrell urging him on, Sobers rediscovered his timing and quickened the tempo, particularly against Johnny Martin. Initially, he was not quite as content against Richie Benaud and survived a confident leg-before wicket appeal to a ball that went periously close to bowling him.

No sooner had Sobers acknowledged the applause for his half-century than he lost Worrell, who attempted to swing Benaud to fine leg but managed only to give Davidson a straightforward catch at a fine leg slip. Sobers was unfazed, however, and in Seymour Nurse found another useful ally. Indeed, Nurse had much of the strike early, and at tea was 31 with Sobers 80 and the total 215.

In his inimitable way, Sobers intensified his assault after the adjournment, being as dismissive of the new ball as he was of the old, and moved quickly to his second century of the series.

Those in the crowd of 37,198 who had seen him fail for 2 and 0 in the first match against New South Wales marvelled at his superlative stroke play and the precision of his placement. And they were speechless when, apparently defeated by a slower delivery from Meckiff, he made a split-second readjustment and gathered six runs from an audacious on-drive into the Sheridan stand.

It is a stroke still spoken about by those who were there.

Three more boundaries — from a hook, cut and cover drive — in the next over compelled Benaud to try Mackay in place of Meckiff, who had conceded 31 in three overs. Benaud shared the workload with Mackay, and to his undisguised relief ended the spectacular sixth wicket stand when he drew a defensive error from Nurse outside the off stump and Bob Simpson took the catch at slip. Nurse had played serviceably for his 43, and with Sobers had added a telling 128 in just 112 minutes at the most opportune time.

Not long after Sobers forced Mackay through the covers to reach 150 the sky darkened, a wind howled and umpires Colin Egar and Colin Hoy had no option but to call a premature halt to proceedings. It was an untimely interruption for Sobers, who had been in irresistible touch after tea, adding 70 in 90 minutes and lifting the total to 5–303.

Benaud's dismissal of Joe Solomon in the morning gave Simpson his fourth catch of the innings and precipitated a startling collapse. Sobers departed without any addition to the score and the tail followed in quick order, the last five wickets falling for 10 runs.

Sobers, who had batted outside the popping crease in the hope of changing Davidson's length finally fell to his great adversary when he miscued a pull and offered a return catch. It seemed a tame conclusion to a wonderful innings of 168. He had held centre stage for four and a half hours and had struck 25 boundaries and the incredible six.

Davidson was again in grand form with another five wickets while Benaud, whose left wrist was bandaged after a heavy fall

Les Favell sweeps before animated keeper Gerry Alexander. For the first time the slow men had an emphatic say in proceedings with Richie Benaud, Alf Valentine and Lance Gibbs each taking eight wickets for the match. *News Ltd*

attempting a return catch the previous day, had provided splendid support.

Australia's pursuit began badly. Simpson fell to a glorious catch by Kanhai at fine leg slip to Wes Hall and Neil Harvey, taking guard outside leg stump, failed to get across to Hall and was smartly caught by Sobers at third slip. When Alf Valentine bowled Colin McDonald for 34, Australia were a very vulnerable 3–65.

The pitch became steadily more responsive to spin, and Valentine and Lance Gibbs, who had been preferred to the disappointing and brooding Sonny Ramadhin, were increasingly more difficult to resist. To add to the challenge for the Australians, Worrell also called upon Sobers to bowl spin.

Only O'Neill played with a measure of confidence, until he was bowled by Sobers for a fine 71 with 10 boundaries in 142 minutes.

Again, to the disappointment of the big crowd of 44,331, poor light brought an abrupt end to the day's proceedings, and again it was the West Indies who were disadvantaged, with Davidson and Mackay scrambling to keep their wickets intact.

Resuming on Monday at 5–172 the Australian lower order capitulated just as dramatically as the West Indians two days earlier. Indeed, they lost their last five wickets for eight runs, with Gibbs, in his first appearance against Australia, dismissing Mackay, Martin and Wally Grout in four balls.

Gibbs bowled with great imagination and variation for figures of 3–46 from 23 overs while Valentine finished with 4–67 from 24.2 overs. The critics of the day observed that Valentine looked a more accomplished and dangerous bowler from over the wicket.

With Australia 137 in arrears Benaud had no option but to employ a fine leg and third man as Davidson bowled at pace and made the ball swing and lift. But even without an intimidating field he promptly had Hunte caught chest-high by O'Neill at third slip, and Kanhai caught off the glove by Martin at backward short leg. And Sobers was adjudged by umpire Hoy to have feathered one to Grout.

Peerless all-rounder. Garfield Sobers bowling wrist spin at Sydney. *ABC*

Every day, virtually every session, the series had provided another twist, and at 3–22 there seemed the prospect of further convulsions. Smith and Worrell, however, were intent on putting the match beyond the reach of the Australians, and played with great enterprise. Their fourth wicket stand of 101 occupied just 70 minutes — the second 50 coming in 30 minutes and being heralded by a six from Worrell off Martin which landed on the lawn in front of the ladies' stand.

With Martin giving away 37 runs in four overs, Benaud returned to the front line and immediately terminated Smith's finest innings for the series at 55.

As Davidson was hors de combat with a hamstring injury and Meckiff was sidelined with a back complaint,

Benaud's resourcefulness as a leader was sorely tested. Needing to slow the run-rate, he bowled in tandem with Mackay, and between them they accounted for Nurse and Solomon. But still Worrell prospered — until he was controversially given out leg before wicket to Benaud for a splendid 82, with 11 fours and a six, that had taken 3 hours and 18 minutes. Among the most technically perfect and elegant batsmen of any time, one cover drive Worrell played against Davidson brought gasps and an ovation from the crowd. Such was his majesty.

At stumps the West Indies were 7–179, 316 runs ahead.

In the absence of Davidson and Meckiff, Mackay took the new ball and shared it with Benaud, who made a rare appearance in the guise of a slow-medium seam bowler. But it was in his traditional and pure role that he removed Gibbs, who scored only 18 but stayed with the ever-reliable Gerry Alexander for 91 minutes and helped him add 74 for the eighth wicket.

Making light of a leg muscle complaint, Alexander then added 69 for the ninth wicket with the flamboyant Hall and 17 for the 10th wicket with Valentine, completing the only Test century of his fine career along the way. His 108 took 212 minutes and included nine fours and a six.

An hour before tea the Australians began the futile pursuit of a colossal 464 runs.

After Simpson was yorked by Sobers for 12, McDonald was joined by Harvey, who was intent on atoning for a disappointing campaign which had produced just 41 runs in five hands. When he lost McDonald he found a reliable partner in O'Neill, and in time the runs flowed freely. By stumps they had added an unbroken 99 in 89 minutes and the requirement had fallen to 282 runs.

Worrell opened the final day, which was unseasonably cool and showery, with his spinners and, as it happened, did not have to call upon Hall.

O'Neill had no sooner posted the 100 partnership for the third wicket when Harvey pulled a hamstring. After a delay for Simpson to re-emerge as a runner, Harvey, in pain and severely restricted in his movement, lunged at Gibbs and was brilliantly caught by Sobers at extra cover. He had made 85 (with nine fours)

Alan Davidson (left) and Ken 'Slasher' Mackay resume on the third day with Australia floundering at 5-172 in response to the West Indies 339. *News Ltd*

Powerful Seymour Nurse leans back and across to cut Ken Mackay ahead of point. Bob Simpson (left) and Wally Grout look on.
News Ltd

in three hours, and recaptured some of his imposing touch.

Australia's hopes of denying the West Indies a deserved victory went with Harvey. O'Neill finally departed for 70, and for the second time in the match the Australian lower order capitulated. Of the last seven only Benaud reached double figures. Australia lost their last seven wickets for 50 and the West Indies triumphed by 222 runs.

During the damp morning Gibbs took 5–27 from 13 overs to boast the match figures of 8–112 from 49 overs, while Valentine could happily point to a match analysis of 8–153 from 49.4 overs.

For the moment, at least, the West Indies had overcome their distrust of one of the world's great cricket grounds.

ON REFLECTION

IAN MECKIFF: I wasn't bowling very well, which seemed to be my wont in the series. I was bowling to Sobers with a second new ball and I bowled him a slower ball about three balls beforehand and he didn't pick it up very quickly. So I thought I'd give him another one. So I bowled him another slow ball and he changed his mind and suddenly rocked back and hit me over mid-wicket for six, landing on the asphalt that is now the Churchill Brewongle stand. I said: 'Oh, thanks very much.' It was one of the most amazing shots you could ever see. Davo [Alan Davidson] said afterwards: 'You just stuffed up the new ball beautifully didn't you!'

NEIL HARVEY: Sobers went to go forward, changed his mind for some reason, went back and the ball disappeared over the mid-on boundary for six off the back foot. Now, that is a pretty exceptional shot. It's the only time I've ever seen it done, actually, something like that.

WES HALL: He [Sobers] sort of pushed forward to a Meckiff slower ball and obviously didn't get to the pitch. If you beat a great player I think that is good enough. But when he comes on to the back foot and hits you for six, I mean, that's something else.

GARFIELD SOBERS: I don't recall many innings because I play the game on the field when I'm there and soon as I finish I kind of forget about it and go on to the next one and think about the next one. But I remember one particular instance, incident, and it happened to Meckiff. I think he'd come back on with the second new ball or something like that late in the day. I was blasting away because I started to see the ball again and I was playing my shots. Ian ran up and bowled me a slower delivery and he had me completely beaten on the front foot. I thought quickly: well, if I'm going to be out I'm going to make sure that it's going to be a very high catch and whoever gets on it is going to be circling it for a while and give me a 50-50 chance. I came back on to the back foot with the same stroke and follow through and I think it finished in the door behind the bowler's arm in a little pub (in the Sheridan stand). He said, 'Bloody good shot, but why did you have to do it to me!' I remember replying, 'Ian, it was either your or I, so I had to take the chance.'

WES HALL: I think the people of Australia began to say, hey, we've got a good series on our hands.

GARFIELD SOBERS: I was a hundred and something not out overnight and as I came out the next day Frank said to me: 'I want you to cut out the hook shot.' Now, I don't know for what reason. Alan Davidson bowled me a bouncer and I got caught in two minds. I was in no-man's land and the ball hit the top edge and flew in the air and I was caught and bowled.

ALF VALENTINE: They were planning to send Lance back home because he had pulled this leg muscle. We had a masseur 'Manny' Alves on the tour and he worked on Lance, worked on him until he got that leg back.

GERRY ALEXANDER: It was the first time I had made three figures in a first-class match. I was fortunate, as Lance [Gibbs] and others have reminded me; if they hadn't stayed at the wicket I would never have done it.

ALAN DAVIDSON: Gerry scored an enormous amount of runs in the series. I don't think he failed. He was a real thorn in our side. By the second or third Test we realised we had a bloke that could actually bat higher on the list. He went in at seven but really he should have been batting at five. He was such a fighter, too. And a real dour sort of fighter as well. And this apart from being a great keeper.

LANCE GIBBS: The tied Test as well as the win at Sydney had lifted the team, and I think we performed even better as we went on.

GARFIELD SOBERS: After the Test match in Sydney we definitely thought we had a very good chance of winning the series and turning the tables on Australia. That we were beginning to become a team to reckon with gave us the kind of encouragement and enthusiasm to go out there and play well.

GERRY ALEXANDER: One of the more outstanding memories I have of this game was when Frank Worrell drove Davidson through the covers for four. And no one moved. But everybody in the ground stood up and applauded. I remember Gerry Gomez, our manager, screaming in our dressingroom because he had never seen a more beautiful shot; one shot for four! And he looked out at the crowd and said: 'You can go home now; you've seen it all.'

ALAN DAVIDSON: Take all the technical perfections that can be created at any one shot at any one time in any sport. And that to me was this cover drive he [Worrell] played in Sydney. I thought, gosh, that was some shot.

7

THE CLAW

Not even a reputation for loquaciousness allows irrepressible Alan Davidson to articulate the depth of feeling and affection that existed between the protagonists.

'There was something between the teams which I can't explain to this day,' says Davidson.

The intensity of his enduring relationship with his opposite number, Wes Hall, is among the most powerful symbols of this remarkable series.

'Wes and myself never shake hands. We actually grab one another and hug one another; we actually go into a bear hug and you can feel the emotion. I can feel the emotion of him and I'm sure he can feel the emotion I'm giving back to him.'

Davidson's place among the game's foremost all-rounders was assured after his extraordinary achievements throughout this series. In four Test matches he took a staggering 33 wickets at 18.54 and scored 212 runs at 30.28. The next most productive Australian paceman was Frank Misson, who took nine wickets at 41.44 in three Tests.

Eight years older than Hall, Davidson was 31, and within 26

Left: Alan Davidson has devoted his life to the service of cricket.
Scott Barbour/Allsport

months of retirement (with 186 Test wickets at 20.53), when he finally realised his ambition to play against the West Indies.

Davidson began his first-class career for New South Wales against South Australia at Adelaide in December 1949 at the age of 20 and made such an impression in his first season — 26 wickets at 18.73 — that he toured New Zealand with an Australian second XI early in 1950.

He was chosen for the solitary match against a New Zealand XI and saw his name in headlines when he scored an undefeated 157 and took all 10 wickets in an innings in a second-class match against Wairarapa at Masterton about 75 kilometres northeast of Wellington.

Any secretly harboured ambition to play against John Goddard's West Indies team in Australia in 1951–52 was unrealised as he undertook his apprenticeship in the powerful NSW team, but a splendid 1952–53 season (41 wickets at 26.75) assured him of a place in the Australian team for England in 1953. He played his first Test against England at Trent Bridge, Nottingham the week of his 24th birthday.

Two years later his hopes of playing against the West Indies on Australia's first tour of the Caribbean were dashed when he chipped an ankle bone in the opening tour match against Jamaica at Kingston. To be sidelined for a month and two Test matches was an impossible impediment, especially as Keith Miller, Ray Lindwall, Ron Archer and Bill Johnston were numbered among his team-mates.

In the second half of the 1950s Davidson established himself as an all-rounder of international repute. He was perhaps at the apex of his career in South Africa in 1957–58 when he took 72 wickets at 15.13 (25 wickets at 17.00 in five Tests) and scored 813 runs (with four centuries) at 54.20.

When his chance finally came to play against the West Indies at the start of the tumultuous 1960s, the gods again threatened to shun him. On the eve of the first Test that ultimately was to earn him admission to the pantheon of all-rounders he badly damaged the little finger of his left hand during catching practice.

As well as introducing structured team meetings Benaud started rigorous and comprehensive match-eve practice sessions when he took over the leadership against England in 1958–59.

There was the customary mix of nervous excitement and tension at practice at the Gabba on 8 December, and after an intense net session Benaud began hitting catches to the slippers.

'Richie was a great disciplinarian on the practice,' says

The master left armer at full stride.

Davidson. 'After bowling for about an hour and half Richie is blasting the ball at us from about five yards. As soon as it hit I thought something was broken. It cracked and I knew it was something really bad, so I just walked straight away from him.

'He said: "Where do you think you're going?" I said I was going to put some ice on this finger if he didn't mind. By the time I got into the rooms I couldn't bend the finger.'

Even allowing for Davidson's renowned tendency to exaggerate the extent of injury or ailment, both Benaud and the chairman of selectors, Sir Donald Bradman could have made good use of worry beads.

Sir Donald told Davidson: 'Well, we'll need you tomorrow. We'd better look at it in the morning.'

'I went to practice in the morning and I couldn't bend the top joint at all. Still to this day I can't bend the top joint. Of course, he said it was OK to play.'

And so it was. Davidson gave arguably the greatest of his many superlative all-round performances to become the first cricketer to aggregate 100 runs and take 10 wickets in a Test match. Batting at number seven he scored 44 and 80, and finished with a match analysis of 11–222 from 54.6 eight-ball overs.

At the height of the celebrations after the match, Sir Donald mischievously confided to Davidson: 'By the way, Alan, you couldn't break your finger before every game, could you?'

'That's a typical Bradman remark which I love,' says Davidson.

There was not, however, the same flippancy when a hamstring injury prevented Davidson playing in the fourth Test match at Adelaide.

Wes Hall, himself destined for greatness as a fast bowler, also carried all before him in Brisbane. Batting at number 10 he scored 50 and 18 and finished with match figures of 9–203 from 48.2 overs.

Between them they accounted for 20 of the 35 wickets that fell to bowlers in the tied Test. And it was from this extraordinary

The Claw, the consummate all-rounder. Alan Davidson strikes a classical pose at the now defunct SCG number two ground. *ABC*

shared experience that their close friendship was born.

They quickly discovered cricket was not their only sporting interest, and references to form on the track soon extended beyond the boundary to the country's metropolitan and provincial racecourses and trotting tracks.

Given that playing commitments generally made it impossible for them to go racing on Saturday or public holidays Davidson and Hall and other keen punters within their ranks happily turned their attention to harness racing. Within half an hour of play ending in Sydney, Davidson and Hall, Cammie Smith and others would be in the Davidson family Holden, heading for an evening meeting at Harold Park raceway at inner-suburban Glebe.

Their passion for cricket and racing is undiminished today, and along with rich recollections of summers and races past continues to act as the catalyst for one of cricket's most vibrant and lasting friendships.

Davidson, like Hall, has served cricket throughout his life. On 20 July 2000, 36 days after his 71st birthday, he entered his 31st year as president of New South Wales Cricket (formerly the NSW Cricket Association) and is therefore poised to become the association's longest-serving president since its formation in 1857. (Sydney Smith served from September 1935 to July 1966.)

An ebullient soul, Davidson is renowned for his skill as the host of association functions — especially match-day luncheons. He has been known to make specific and entertaining references by name to 80 or more people, all without a prompter or cue cards.

A life member of the NSWCA, the Sydney Cricket Ground and Sports Ground Trust and the Marylebone Cricket Club, London, Davidson is acknowledged as one of the most distinguished servants of NSW cricket. He was awarded the MBE in 1963 and the AM in 1987.

He acted as a Test selector at one of the most sensitive periods in the history of Australian cricket, being appointed to the panel in 1978 at the height of the World Series Cricket schism and choosing the first teams following reunification in 1979. He continued to serve on the panel until 1984.

That he is a member of the Australian Jockey Club and Sydney Turf Club and a life member of the NSW Trotting Club and Sydney Tattersalls Club reflects his well-documented passion for horse racing. He has also held positions with the Thoroughbred Racing Board of NSW Integrity and Assurance Committee and the NSW Country Racing Development Fund Board.

Davidson also enjoyed a prominent profile as the executive director of the Rothmans Foundation — National Sport Division from 1974 to 1995, and has been conspicuous for community work for the Bradman Trust and Foundation, the Red Cross, the ANZAC Foundation Council, Legacy and the Child Accident Prevention Foundation of Australia Committee.

The prospect of Hall returning to Australia for the 40th anniversary celebrations of the goodwill series ensured that Davidson approached his 31st year as supremo of NSW cricket with youthful and infectious enthusiasm.

8

EXTENDED FAMILY

He cannot remember the name of the boys' home he visited in Sydney this unforgettable summer, but Alf Valentine has never forgotten the boys' faces. Just months into his 31st year, Valentine was disturbed by the boys' stories of dislocation and displacement, but he cheered them up the best he could with his flashing smile, ready wit and cricket conversation.

At the same time he made a solemn if silent pledge to one day devote his life to the care of disadvantaged youth. And he honoured his word, as his host of admirers knew he would. Val, as he is affectionately known, is a good and giving man.

Since moving from his native Jamaica to live in the USA in 1978, Val and his second wife Jacquelyn have been surrogate parents to hundreds of 'adjudicated children', to use the vernacular of the US justice system. In essence, these are abandoned, neglected or abused children between the ages of 5 and 18 who are in need of special care and counselling while their parents or guardians are in jail and/or being rehabilitated.

Formally classified as youth residential co-ordinators, at any

Left: Alf Valentine being feted at a ceremony on his home ground at Sabina Park, Kingston, Jamaica in recent years.
Gordon Brooks

given time they can have as many as 12 young people in their care at Great Oaks Village, Orlando, which is run and principally funded by the Orange County government in Florida. The Valentines can reflect on some heart-warming successes, but there have been gut-wrenching failures, too.

There is considerable laughter when Valentine confesses that neither he nor Jacquelyn, a native Floridian who graduated with a masters degree in business at the age of 48, is daunted by the size of their extended family. After all, at last count, Val's four daughters by his late first wife, Gwendolyn, had provided him with 11 grandchildren. At mid-May 2000, there are also two great grandchildren.

While there has been speculation that international cricket will be played at a purpose-built stadium at Disney World, Orlando early in the 21st century, there is little awareness of the game outside the expatriate West Indian community in Florida, and Valentine uses his trusty short-wave radio and the Internet to remain abreast of happenings throughout the cricket world.

Commitment to work and to regular and long walks on the beach near his home at Daytona Beach Shores ensured that Valentine was especially healthy in mind and body as he entered his eighth decade in April 2000.

Given that a chronic finger injury and indifferent form had prevented him from playing regularly towards the end of the 1950s, he considered himself fortunate to be chosen for his second trip to Australia. Frank Worrell, a friend and staunch supporter, and Sonny Ramadhin were the only other survivors of John Goddard's 1951–52 team, the second West Indies team to tour Australia.

Valentine's appearance in the first Test at Brisbane was only his third since the fourth and final Test against New Zealand at Auckland in March 1956, and his first since January 1958, when Hanif Mohammad batted for 16 hours and 10 minutes for 337 to inspire an extraordinary draw for Pakistan in Barbados.

Tall, lean and always wearing glasses, Valentine earned instant celebrity barely six weeks after his 20th birthday when he returned the match figures of 11–204 from 106 overs in his Test debut against England at Old Trafford, Manchester.

As it happened, England still won the match comfortably after an hour's play on the fourth day, but it was their only success for the series. The West Indies triumphed in the next three Tests, signalling the emergence of a new power in the game, and Valentine and Ramadhin were feted as spinners of rare ability.

Valentine took 33 wickets at 20.42 and Ramadhin, his senior by 363 days, 26 wickets at 23.23. Their success vindicated the selectors, who had shown considerable prescience choosing them — Valentine was promoted after taking just two wickets (at 95 runs each) in two first-class matches in the Caribbean.

The series success was a seminal moment in the evolution of West Indies cricket, and moved Lord Beginner to compose a famous calypso which remains a precious part of the lore of the game:

Cricket, lovely cricket

At Lord's where I saw it

Yardley tried his best

But West Indies won the Test

With those two little pals of mine

Ramadhin and Valentine.

Fifteen months later he enhanced his reputation in Australia, taking 24 wickets at 28.79 as the West Indies squandered priceless opportunities and lost 4–1 a series which at times was within their reach.

He then took eight wickets in the West Indies' first two Tests against New Zealand so, at the age of 21, could point to 65 wickets at 23.35 in 11 Tests on his first two tours.

Over the next 10 years Valentine played another 25 Tests, completing his career with figures of 139 wickets at 30.32. He made his farewell appearance against India in front of his home crowd at Sabina Park, Kingston in April 1962. He toured England for a third time in 1963 but did not play in a Test.

On the rare occasions when he sees his cricket contempo-

Val, as he is affectionately known, weaving his magic at practice in 1961. *News Ltd*

raries, conversation invariably turns to the goodwill tour of 1960–61. Although he was then in the twilight of his international career and had played only sporadically during the previous four and a half years, Valentine was tireless and uncomplaining in his endeavours.

As a senior professional it was his duty to be unstinting in his support for his friend Worrell on and off the ground, and by the end of the tour he had bowled more than anyone else — 39 wickets at 28.87 coming from 376.7 overs in 11 first-class matches. Lance Gibbs and Garfield Sobers were the only others to bowl more than 350 overs and Wes Hall was the only more successful bowler, with 40 wickets at 27.72 from 260.4 overs in 12 matches.

That he had such a productive tour was, in part, due to help he received from Benaud, who magnanimously shared a trade secret.

Like Valentine, Benaud struggled through the late 1950s to treat and protect fingers badly damaged from years of bowling — the seam would cut through the skin and do serious, perhaps irreparable, damage. Benaud was at his wits' end when he happened into Ivan James' chemist shop in Timaru during Australia's short tour of New Zealand in 1957.

James instantly recognised Benaud and said he believed he could treat his fingers with a concoction that he had successfully used to assist ex-servicemen suffering from leg ulcers. Benaud left the shop with the ingredients and a piece of paper with the following instructions written on it:

OILY CALAMINE LOTION BPC '54

BORACIC ACID POWDER

Rub the lotion into the wound and then dab off the oil which comes to the surface.

Rub in the boracic acid power so that it forms a waxy filling in the wound.

Keep doing this as much as possible and definitely whenever there is a recurrence of the skin tearing. Make sure you keep the waxy substance filling the hole all the time.

Over the years Benaud has said unequivocally that James was responsible for saving his bowling career.

That Benaud provided Valentine with the concoction showed not only the fraternal spirit between the two teams, but also the level of the friendships which flourished throughout the summer.

'I remember Richie showed me what to do in Sydney. It was like placing a plastic film over it to form a little skin.' Valentine remembered.

While Valentine did not derive as many benefits from the treatment as Benaud, he was able to maintain a workload far beyond the expectations of his doctor in Jamaica. And for that he was most grateful.

Perhaps Benaud felt that in some way he was in Valentine's debt. After all, Val was Benaud's first Test wicket — his only wicket from his first spell of 4.3 overs at the Sydney Cricket Ground on 29 January 1952.

Lance Gibbs walks on air as he claims the first hat-trick in Australia — West Indies cricket. (top) Ken Mackay is adjudged leg before wicket; (centre) Wally Grout is smartly caught by Garfield Sobers lunging forward at leg-slip; and, (bottom) Frank Mission is bowled by a markedly quicker delivery. *News Ltd*

9

BRUISE OF HONOUR

Fourth Test

Adelaide: 27, 28, 30, 31 January, 1 February

Next to Ron Lovitt's wonderful photograph of Ian Meckiff failing to make his ground in the tied Test match, the most enduring image of the series is Lindsay Kline defending his wicket with 10 West Indians squatting under his bat. Yet it was his batting partner, the gum-chewing anti-hero Ken Mackay, who was the architect of the most famous resistance movement organised in the annals of the Australian game. The two left-handers drew strength from each other, and in the end defied the might of the West Indians for 110 minutes to ensure that Australia did not fall behind in the series and so lose their last chance of winning it.

Mackay famously took the last ball of the match from Wes Hall on his body.

Often ridiculed for his dourness and tedious slow scoring, Mackay on this occasion was a bruised and unbowed national hero. After such an intense fight for survival, Mackay was not prepared to put his bat anywhere near the last ball. Renowned for his love of the team and team values, he simply raised his bat as though to shoulder arms and took the sickening blow in the midriff.

It was an act of great courage that has become a special part of the history of the game. As disconsolate as they were, West Indian fieldsmen were among those who helped Mackay make his way slowly and painfully through the excited back-slapping mob to the grandstand.

Once seated in the dressingroom, Richie Benaud went to him and said, 'Well done.'

'Thanks, mate,' came the reply.

Nothing more was said.

It said much for the West Indians that they accepted the result of the match without rancour. To a man they were convinced

Frank Misson surveys his broken wicket as Lance Gibbs completes the 16th hat-trick in Test cricket. Taken by amateur photographer Albert Devonshire this is the first known image of the historic moment taken from square with the wicket. Devonshire's nephew Darren Silva recently ensured the photograph reached the museum at Adelaide Oval. Wicketkeeper Gerry Alexander is flanked by Garfield Sobers and Joe Solomon.
Albert Devonshire

Mackay had been caught by Garfield Sobers at silly mid-off to Frank Worrell when he was 17 and more than an hour before he so dramatically put his body on the line. However, umpire Colin Egar was unconvinced, and when the fieldsmen finally realised they needed to make a formal appeal, he refused it.

In the circumstances, the draw was as good as victory for the Australians, who had been seriously weakened by the withdrawal of Alan Davidson, Ian Meckiff and Neil Harvey because of injury. The absence of Davidson was especially crushing, given he had taken 27 wickets in the first three Tests.

Worrell won the toss for the third time and immediately consigned Australia's new opening bowlers Frank Misson, in his second Test, and Des Hoare, on debut, to purgatory. As Rohan Kanhai and Worrell atoned for the early loss of Conrad Hunte, Cammie Smith and Sobers (who was bowled by a gem of a delivery from Benaud which turned, lifted and clipped his off bail), the temperature reached 105.7°F (40.9°C).

Kanhai, in his own mind at least vying with Sobers for the mantle of pre-eminent batsman within the team, played with a freedom and confidence that compelled Benaud to review his modus operandi and rearrange the bowling order. He and Lindsay Kline worked in tandem before the second drinks break of the session, but neither could curb the rampant Kanhai.

Given the oppressive conditions it was an extraordinary achievement for the West Indies to score 133 in the first two-hour session — Kanhai contributing 76.

The lunch respite further fortified both batsmen. Kanhai resumed by lifting Hoare into the members' area, while Worrell had to replace his bat after one savage offering against Hoare. In the first five overs after the adjournment they added 46 runs. Benaud was still unable to stem the flow.

In the end, the fierce heat also took its toll on the batsman. Kanhai lapsed in concentration and was smartly caught by Bob Simpson at slip to Benaud for 117. This innings was a tour de force by Kanhai which lasted barely 150 minutes and included 14 fours and two sixes.

Worrell, 11 years older than Kanhai, found the heat even

more enervating, and after abandoning his cap for a white washing hat — a most unusual occurrence — his stroke play, which had been so forceful and authoritative, suddenly became languid and unconvincing. Team masseur 'Manny' Alves endeavoured to reinvigorate him during the tea break, but after being missed by Norm O'Neill in the covers to Benaud on 62, he finally gave Hoare his second — and, as it happened, last — Test wicket at 71.

Seymour Nurse made some fine offerings before falling to a remarkable return catch by the indefatigable Misson, but the redoubtable and consistent Gerry Alexander remained unbeaten on 38 with the West Indies 7–348 at the end of a hot, memorable day.

Not even Adelaide's cursed hot north wind disrupted Alexander's progress on Saturday morning as he recorded his fourth half-century for the series and, with Lance Gibbs, added 59 for the eighth wicket. In the end the West Indies reached 393 in seven hours and eight minutes. In the circumstances, the Australians did well to bowl at an average of fractionally more than an over every five minutes.

Frank Misson dives full length to his left to hold an exceptional return catch from the flailing bat of Seymour Nurse. *Fairfax*

To the great disappointment of his home crowd, the promotion of Les Favell from five to opener was unsuccessful, and it was left to Simpson (at four) to provide early support for Colin McDonald. But not even the abatement of the unpleasant northerly made their task any easier against the guileful Gibbs and the aggressive Hall, and there were few attacking strokes between lunch and tea as the score reached 103.

McDonald added 10 runs after the adjournment before being splendidly caught by Hunte on the fence behind square leg to Gibbs. Peter Burge, summoned for the first time in the series, joined Simpson.

Burge played with poise and power against both Gibbs and Alf Valentine, and in time Worrell was left with no option but to reintroduce the trusty Hall to proceedings.

However, when the new ball was due Worrell surprised many by sharing it with Sobers and not Hall. It was a successful ploy, with Burge bowled by Sobers just before stumps prompting Benaud to move up the order as nightwatchman alongside Simpson on 85 and the total at 4–221.

The body language of the West Indian fieldsmen suggests Lindsay Kline was fortunate to survive this incident against the bowling of Frank Worrell. The slippers have launched into something of a jig as keeper Gerry Alexander dives to make a save. *News Ltd*

Simpson spent the rest day pondering the possibility of reaching his maiden Test century, but again it was not to be — Hall had him caught at the wicket by Alexander without a run being added.

Benaud then elicited solid support from Mackay and they carefully negotiated a double bowling change by Worrell to advance the score to 281. Then Gibbs added another dimension to the match and series by achieving a hat-trick.

The guns from the nearby Torrens parade ground that blasted an Australia Day salute had barely fallen silent when Mackay was given out leg before wicket. Wally Grout was then beautifully caught at leg slip by Sobers and Misson was bowled by a quicker delivery. Gibbs, arms outstretched, leapt high in excitement and was effusively congratulated by his team-mates. It was the first hat-trick in a Test in Australia since Hugh Trumble performed the feat against England in 1903–04, and the first in competition between the West Indies and Australia. The holiday crowd gave Gibbs a rousing reception.

Benaud had witnessed the procession from 22 yards and could scarcely conceal his alarm with Australia still 112 runs adrift.

As Ken Mackay and Lindsay Kline dug in for their renowned last-wicket stand, the West Indians became increasingly frustrated and perhaps erred in bowling their overs too quickly. Despite his modest credentials as a batsman Kline was imperturbable even when confronted by all fieldsmen crouched under his bat. On this occasion Wes Hall is the bowler retrieving the ball at Kline's feet. *News Ltd*

However, Hoare showed that he had the stomach for a fight, and supported his skipper with such aplomb that they added 85 for the ninth wicket in a little over 100 minutes, before Sobers got one through his defences. It was a stirring performance by Hoare, and the West Indians graciously joined in the warm applause as he left the ground with Australia just 27 runs in arrears.

While he had neither their technique nor reputation, Smith could be as devastating a batsman as his celebrated team-mates when his high-risk game gelled. On this occasion he was merciless against a weary Hoare and Misson, and thrashed 10 boundaries in 46 before driving Mackay to Hoare at mid-on.

While Hunte did not begin with his customary confidence, the opening partnership was worth 66 and provided Kanhai with an ideal stage on which to again showcase his thrilling stroke play. He immediately picked up his cue, and although he had given Hunte an hour's start, by the time the West Indies were 1–150 he had outscored him by 15, to be 59. With two days' remaining, the West Indies were in an impregnable position leading by 177 runs with nine wickets in hand.

Kanhai reached his second century of the match, but at considerable cost to the team cause. Having reached 99, he played Misson quietly to the off and called Hunte for a single. Misson, a fine athlete, followed through at pace, made a fine interception and dived forward spectacularly, throwing down the stumps with an underarm throw.

Clearly Kanhai was distressed by his impetuous and thoughtless action, and after late-cutting Hoare for his century in 163 minutes he was marooned on 103 for three quarters of an hour. Knowing that he was only the second West Indian — Clyde Walcott was the other — to score a century in each innings of a Test against Australia would not have lightened his burden.

Hunte, who with Kanhai had added 163 for the second wicket, had himself seemed destined for a hundred. Sensing how remorseful Kanhai would feel, Hunte endeavoured to catch his attention and exhort him to maintain his concentration. To the crowd's amusement Hunte became disorientated, and made to leave the ground through the wrong gate.

However, despite Hunte's wholehearted reassurances, Kanhai failed to prosper, and soon after lunch was adjudged leg before wicket to Benaud while trying to force through mid-wicket. While Kanhai received another ovation, much of the applause was reserved for his conqueror, who joined Alec Bedser, Ray Lindwall and Clarrie Grimmett as the only bowlers to have taken 200 wickets in Test matches.

The celebrations had scarcely died down when Misson thrillingly repeated his dismissal of Hunte to account for Sobers and Benaud struck again, removing Nurse.

If there was any unease in the West Indies camp that a handsome advantage was being squandered at 5–275, it was not apparent in the batting of Worrell and Alexander. Again relishing the responsibility of leadership they cut, drove and pulled at will, and their hundred partnership for the sixth wicket came in less than even time.

When Worrell fell for 53 — his fifth half-century of the series — speculation intensified as to the timing of his declaration. It came 45 minutes before the close, after Alexander, with an undefeated 87, took the score to 6–432, leaving Australia the impossible task of scoring 460 in 395 minutes.

Indeed, any chance Australia had of saving the match seemed to diminish in the frenetic conclusion to the fourth day, when Favell, McDonald and Simpson were dismissed with 31 runs on the board.

Burge and O'Neill opened impressively on the final day, mixing controlled aggression with sound defence.

For the second time in the match Burge fell as he neared a

Thrilling Rohan Kanhai, who was renowned for his robust pulling and sweeping — even after losing his balance — despatches Ken Mackay behind square leg with characteristic ease. Kanhai earned rave reviews for his two centuries in the Adelaide Test.

half-century — this time caught at the wicket attempting to cut a delivery from Valentine that turned and lifted.

Such was Sobers genius as a cricketer, he could compensate for any lapse at one discipline with a telling achievement at another, and his smart and timely return catches to remove O'Neill and Benaud boosted his aggregate of wickets for the match to five.

Mackay, so very nearly caught at leg-slip by Gibbs before he had scored, gained impressive support from the resolute Grout who counter-punched so impressively that Worrell varied his approach by summoning part-time leg-spinner Solomon for three overs. But in the end, it was Worrell himself who removed Grout, and at tea Australia were 7–203.

Immediately after the adjournment Worrell accounted for Hoare and Misson, and with 110 minutes remaining, Kline made his way to the middle.

'Away you go. Don't want to see you until the end of the game,' was Benaud's casual instruction to Kline as he made his way out of the dressingroom. At the time Benaud was heading for the showers, fully anticipating an early departure from the ground.

'OK,' replied Kline, who was rudely taunted for his modest batting ability by some patrons in the members' pavilion as he made his way onto the ground. To the bewilderment of all, Kline honoured his mumbled pledge to his captain and remained with Mackay to the end.

While he went to the Melbourne Cricket Club at the age of 16 as an opening batsman, as an adult he had few pretensions with the bat, going in at seven or eight for Melbourne, at nine or 10 for Victoria and 11 for Australia. Furthermore, the oft-heard stories of his being repeatedly bowled by O'Neill and Martin at the nets shortly before his innings are true. The number of times he was bowled is perhaps exaggerated, though, Kline believing it to be merely eight or ten!

The joy of taking the first hat-trick for Australia in 45 years is not Kline's only precious memory of his 1957–58 tour of South Africa under Ian Craig. The bonding of the Australian team on this visit was powerful, and was further intensified by Benaud when he succeeded the ailing Craig for the 1958–59 Ashes series.

So while the critics may have considered Kline a peripheral player, the Australian team considered him an important member of their community. Mackay, nearly nine years Kline's senior, had taken a particular interest in his fellow left-hander on the South African tour, and had encouraged him to believe he had the capacity to bat defensively.

Soon the West Indies saw the unspoken rapport between these two self-effacing, unassuming men. The longer the stand progressed the more comfortable Kline became, and his greatest discomfort came not from the menace of Hall but from the guile of Sobers bowling his wrist spin. Not only did Sobers possess a wicked wrong'un; he even managed to extract bounce from a fifth day Adelaide pitch.

As news of the extraordinary partnership reached the city, offices and shops emptied, and a small gathering resigned to defeat was soon swollen to a crowd of 13,691 that dared to consider an improbable draw.

Kline, however, was oblivious to the pandemonium around the ground but he was aware of the mounting anxiety among the West Indians who lost some poise by bowling their overs at a frantic pace. At the height of the stand they were bowling some overs in two minutes and 113.1 overs were despatched for the day.

While Kline and Mackay said little, they established some kind of telepathic link as the minutes ticked over agonisingly slowly.

'We had this feeling going on,' recalls Kline, 'even if we didn't speak about it. We were willing each other on. You know, just hang in there; do your best; you're doing OK; that's good; well played. My mind was going through what he did and he was doing the same when I was batting.

'I knew that when I got through that second last over I was not moving from the crease. It didn't matter if he'd called me 10 times I was staying where I'd done my job. And he knew that. And I'm glad he took Hall.'

'Johnnie' Moyes quaintly described Kline as using a straight bat which 'was a pillar of respectability and morality'. Be that as it may, his heroics did not secure his place in the team. It was Kline's 13th and final Test match for Australia.

ON REFLECTION

LANCE GIBBS: I realised Frank Misson coming in was going to push down the line bat and pad. So, I bowled a little seam-up quicky ... zoom ...

RICHIE BENAUD: There was no great excitement for me at the non-striker's end. I was pretty cranky about the whole thing.

ROHAN KANHAI: You don't make a hundred in each innings of a Test every day. It was a special day for me when that happened.

NEIL HARVEY: 'Slasher' would go down probably as one of the best team players I've played with. You could ask 'Slasher' to go out and try and make 50 in 50 minutes, he'd do it, which is against his style of play. Or else you could ask him to go out there and say: 'I want you to stick around for four hours and make 10.' That was his style of play and he could do that. You could ask him to go out and bowl 30 overs, and he'd go and do it. He'd do anything you asked him to do; a tremendous team player and courageous.

JACKIE HANDRIKS: I distinctly recall it was about twenty past four when Kline went out to bat. Of course we were starting to prepare to leave; to pack the bags or whatever you had to do as another 10 minutes it would be all over.

RICHIE BENAUD: We've all seen shots of 'Slasher' [Mackay] leaving the ball go when it is going two inches past the off stump. I cannot recall 'Slasher' being bowled not playing a shot. He just had wonderful judgment.

LANCE GIBBS: When you look at the record of Lindsay Kline, you know, we figured we were home and dried.

GARFIELD SOBERS: At the time you didn't have any worries. Whatever happened you figured that you were going to win this game.

PETER LASHLEY: I could imagine 'Slasher' Mackay batting out. But I couldn't imagine Lindsay Kline batting that period of time.

LINDSAY KLINE:

It was probably a million to one chance that I got through but it did happen. It started in the nets when Norm O'Neill and Johnny Martin took me out for some practice. They bowled to me for about 20 minutes and I was bowled eight to ten times, and I'm playing at balls that I thought were going to turn and they went straight and balls that went straight turned. There was a woman standing behind the nets and she said: 'Well, look, it's a waste of time sending you in, isn't it?' Well, I couldn't disagree with her the way I was batting. When I went into the dressingroom the boys were packing their bags to go home. It didn't give you much confidence. I walked down the stairs and one of the members said 'Last out, ho, ho, ho; it's all up to you now', and the whole stand started to laugh. So I went on my way and it was just one of those days; I was focused and I just concentrated on every ball.

CONRAD HUNTE: We were so convinced it was a perfect catch that we all left the field. We didn't even appeal. When nothing happened and 'Slasher' stayed, then we thought, what's up? So we said: 'Mr Umpire, how's that?' And he said: 'Not out.'

CAMMIE SMITH: There was no doubt in all of our minds that it was a clean catch. There was no doubt.

GARFIELD SOBERS: I remember we started to blow our tops about it. And Frank [Worrell] said, 'Come on, quieten down. If the umpire says that it's not out that's the position.'

LINDSAY KLINE: 'Slasher' was certain it was a bump ball. And I thought it was a bump ball.

BOB SIMPSON: We were square on in Adelaide and had a perfect view of the actual flight of the ball and everything. It never ever occurred to us that it was a catch. And it didn't occur to 'Slasher'. I think what happened was that the West Indies hoped.

LINDSAY KLINE: 'Slasher' just said, 'Keep your head down.' He gave me a lot of confidence. He believed that I could bat defensively. And he said that to me a few times at the nets. 'Slasher' was

the right man for the job. He didn't hassle me with details. We just had a couple of little chats and I think I mumbled 'Yes, OK' and went back to the job. He was a wonderful team man. We got on quite well.

WES HALL: I was criticised for not bowling Kline any bouncers. But I had so often seen batsmen who were very capable of being struck in the head and things like that and I didn't think that to bowl a bouncer was the thing to do. So I kept the ball up and he loved it, and I was criticised for that. But that's fair enough with me. I just didn't think it was the thing to do.

RICHIE BENAUD: We started to get excited about 10 minutes into the last hour.

LINDSAY KLINE: I became quite nervous when we had about 20 minutes to go and then I looked at the clock and I thought, gee, we've come a fair way now and I might get through. That's when I got a little tense.

LINDSAY KLINE: We didn't get together until the dressingroom. We tried to get together, we looked, but there were so many people on the ground. When we found each other it was a very special moment. I don't think we said much; just put our arms around each other and had that wonderful feeling that we did something special for the team.

RICHIE BENAUD: The [hand on the] clock at Adelaide Oval goes down very fast on the right-hand side when it's getting down to the half hour and goes up very slowly. It certainly did in those days. About 10 minutes into the last hour we started to get edgy, and we were very edgy towards the end. There was as much shouting coming from the dressingroom as each ball was negotiated as there was from the members, who normally don't shout about anything.

RICHIE BENAUD: He could easily have had a broken rib it was so bruised. It got him in a nasty spot. But he didn't say much when he came off. He went and sat down and obviously he was in a bit of pain. I said 'Well done.' 'Thanks, mate,' he said. That was it.

BOB SIMPSON: I still have this wonderful mental image of 'Slasher' putting his arms above his head, bat held high and allowing it to hit him in the ribs. That takes a lot of cold courage. To be hit when you're trying to avoid it is acceptable, but when you've got to do that for your team - that's a huge contribution.

10

TWICE IN A LIFETIME

Bob Simpson occupies a unique place in cricket history, and not only because he has served the first-class game in numerous capacities for nearly half a century.

That he is the one person involved in cricket's only tied Test matches is, perhaps, the most startling of all his claims to fame in a life devoted to the game.

On 14 December 1960 he was a novice 24-year-old opening batsman forbidden by superstitious 'Slasher' Mackay to move from his seat on the patio of the Australian dressingroom as his team-mates clawed, scratched and scraped their way towards the 233 runs needed to win the first Test with the West Indies at the Woolloongabba ground, Brisbane.

In the end they made 232 of them.

On 22 September 1986 he was a 50-year-old coach sitting on the edge of his rattan chair in the viewing area outside the Australian dressingroom as his team moved heaven and earth to stop India from scoring the 348 they needed to win the first Test at the MA Chidambaram Stadium, Chepauk in Madras (now Chennai).

Left: Bob Simpson. Cricketer, captain, coach, teacher and troubleshooter.
Scott Barbour/Allsport

In the end they restricted them to 347.

During the intervening 25 years, 9 months, 8 days and 550 Test matches Simpson became one of the most powerful and influential figures in Australian cricket.

An outstanding batsman and slips fieldsman of astonishing virtuosity, he became Australia's 30th captain in 1963 at the age of 27, when he succeeded Richie Benaud, and returned to the helm at the age of 41 in 1977 when the cricket world was split asunder by the World Series Cricket revolution. Subsequently he was a selector and the country's first designated coach for a decade from 1986.

While he had made an impressive Test debut at the age of 21 in Johannesburg in December 1957, Simpson did not begin to establish himself as an elite player until he became an opening batsman against the West Indies in 1960–61.

In the five Tests against South Africa in 1957–58 and in his solitary appearance against England in 1958–59 he batted in the middle and lower order — his customary positions since making his debut for New South Wales in January 1953 at the age of 16 and 355 days.

The strength of the NSW team in the 1950s was so intimidat-

September 22, 1986 and another Test match is tied. Umpire V. Vikram Raju raises his finger to uphold off-spinner Greg Matthews' leg before wicket appeal against Maninder Singh. (Players from left) Matthews (wearing cap), Allan Border, Maninder, keeper Tim Zoehrer, Geoff Marsh, Ravi Shastri and Bruce Reid.
Mala Mukherjee

ing that Simpson believed his career could be significantly advanced by playing elsewhere, and in 1956–57 he headed across the Nullarbor Plain to play for Western Australia, which had been admitted to the Sheffield Shield competition in 1947–48.

His instinct proved correct, and a solid season at number three (572 runs at 47.66) was sufficient to earn him selection first for the Australian tour of New Zealand early in 1957 and, ultimately, for five Tests in South Africa seven months later.

He was, however, required for only one of Australia's next 13 Tests, and was overlooked for Benaud's dramatic pioneering visit to Pakistan and India in 1959–60.

Simpson boldly confronted his deficiencies at Test match level, and on the advice of Neil Harvey decided to try his hand as an opening batsman with Accrington in 1959.

He made the transition easily, as was graphically demonstrated on his return to Australia when he amassed 902 runs at a phenomenal 300.66 opening in six innings for Western Australia. And for good measure he topped the averages — with 518 runs at 74.00 — on the Australian Second XI in New Zealand early in 1960.

It was, of course, one thing to prosper in Shield cricket and against the modest attacks encountered in New Zealand, but another altogether to confront the might of Wes Hall.

However, in the absence of Hall, who was rested from the first first-class game of the tour because of ankle soreness, Simpson drew first blood, in the figurative sense, scoring 87 and an undefeated 221, and Western Australia won by 94 runs.

Hall returned to the fray the following week against an Australian XI.

We'd heard a lot about Wes Hall, but we hadn't really seen him and we were playing on a bouncy wicket. Colin McDonald took strike and obviously we were watching as Wes raced in and let the first one go. Colin ducked under it and it took off and went over the head of Gerry Alexander and one bounce into the sightscreen. Colin looked up and said: 'Oh, shit!' I think that set the whole tone.

Simpson had scored so heavily over the previous 12 months that his reinstatement to the Test team was inevitable, and he and

McDonald were reunited for the first Test in Brisbane.

Intent on re-establishing his Test career, Simpson maintained his touch and bore the brunt of Hall's hostility. He was eight runs short of his first Test century when Sonny Ramadhin bowled him. While he fell to Hall for a duck in the second innings, Simpson proved his mettle and garnered sufficient confidence for a prosperous series: 445 runs at 49.44, second only to Norm O'Neill (522 runs at 52.20).

In Adelaide he batted at four, in a rearranged order, and in the second innings of the final Test, at Melbourne, again failed by just eight runs to reach his maiden hundred, after carrying out — to the letter — daring instructions from Benaud to pound a weary Hall.

He may not have been so accepting of his misfortune had he realised it would take another 23 Tests over 3 years, 5 months and 8 days before he realised his goal, at Old Trafford, Manchester. When he finally reached the mark in his 52nd innings he was unconquerable, and added two more hundreds before being dismissed for 311 in 12 hours and 42 minutes.

Another nine centuries followed over his next 30 Tests — two in his second incarnation as captain. At 41 years and 360 days he is the oldest Australian to have scored a century in a home Test. In the end, he also had the remarkable distinction of scoring hundreds in successive innings at Adelaide 10 years apart.

Just as it had begun, his Test career concluded offshore — at Sabina Park, Kingston, Jamaica on 3 May 1978, three months to the day after his 42nd birthday and 20 years 4 months and 10 days since he had walked onto the Wanderers ground, Johannesburg behind his 22-year-old captain, Ian Craig.

Simpson retired as Australia's longest-serving captain — with 12 wins, 12 losses and 15 draws from his 39 outings — a distinction which subsequently belonged to Greg Chappell and then to the indestructible Allan Border, whose 93 matches at the helm is a world record.

However, his leadership role in Australian cricket did not end with his retirement as a player. Eight years after his second retirement he again responded to the cry for help from the game's

Bob Simpson, aged 20, at the Sydney Cricket Ground nets but representing Western Australia in November 1956. *ABC*

governors, and at the age of 50 embarked on his third career with the Australian team — this time as coach.

In 1986 Australian cricket was bankrupt of imagination, inspiration and instruction. And resources. It had no sooner learned to manage the residue of resentment from the tumultuous World Series Cricket schism than it was confronted by dissidents seduced by the rand of the old South Africa.

Simpson, who places great store in the game's traditional values, was appalled at what he termed the breakdown of Australian cricket culture, and roundly charged World Series cricketers with abrogating their responsibilities to the country's emerging first-class cricketers. Clearly not all the resentment had dissipated.

With the support of Border, who initially was a reluctant and diffident captain, Simpson re-educated, reconstructed and reinvigorated the Australian team and established an imposing benchmark for his counterparts around the world and for his successors, Geoff Marsh and John Buchanan.

In his time as coach Australia spectacularly regained the Ashes in England in 1989 — a prize which remained in their possession heading into the 2001 campaign — won the fourth World Cup as 16–1 outsiders at Calcutta in 1987 and reached the final of the sixth World Cup at Lahore in 1996.

Furthermore, with Mark Taylor at the helm, Australia won in the Caribbean in 1995 for the first time in 22 years, thereby regaining the Frank Worrell Trophy, which had been the property of the West Indies since Simpson's official Australian team was overwhelmed in 1978.

His time as coach was not without controversy. While his methods were successful — particularly his emphasis on training regimens — his manner could be irritating, and his predilection for the game's politics and attendant intrigues often confounded and alienated players, officials and media representatives alike.

Nor was he averse to stinging and sometimes uncharitable criticism about the mood, mentality and methodology of cricket outside Australia — particularly in the Caribbean and on the Indian subcontinent, where he was later to coach.

Certainly he could never have imagined, during that happy,

uncomplicated summer of 1960–61, that his future associations with West Indian cricket would be so rancorous.

Indeed, neither Simpson nor Garfield Sobers, Worrell's successor, were able to rekindle the joyful spirit of the 1960–61 series when contact was renewed in the Caribbean four years later. This was a series blighted by the controversy surrounding the legitimacy of the bowling action of the Barbadian fast bowler Charlie Griffith and the reliance of the West Indians on short-pitched bowling.

To add insult to injury, the Australians failed their first defence of the Frank Worrell Trophy and lost the series 2–1.

Simpson's disappointment was just as acute 13 years later when his raw, naive but kosher team was overwhelmed 3–1 as the international cricket community endeavoured to grasp the consequences of the breach which had torn the game apart.

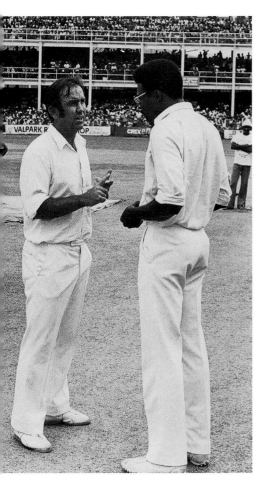

Chewing the fat. Bob Simpson in his second incarnation as Australian captain with the West Indies' longest-serving skipper, Clive Lloyd at Queen's Park Oval, Port of Spain in Trinidad. *Patrick Eagar*

Another 13 years hence saw coach Simpson the butt for a tirade of quite personal criticism by West Indies captain Viv Richards, who clearly had harboured ill-feelings since 1978.

Consequently, the triumph of 1995 provided him with enormous satisfaction. The following year, however, when the Australian Cricket Board decided against renewing his contract, he angrily aired conspiracy theories and named journalists.

In all probability Simpson will always receive mixed reviews, but the fact remains that the value of his contribution to Australian cricket is incalculable.

11

OUT OF DARKNESS INTO LIGHT

The spiritual awakening of Conrad Hunte during the 1960–61 series represents one of the most stirring and inspiring chapters in the history of cricket between Australia and the West Indies.

A consummate and ambitious 28-year-old in just his third year in the Test match arena, Hunte's life was transformed by his exposure to the philosophy of Moral Rearmament, a global Christian movement. As the tour neared its emotional climax in the crowded streets of Melbourne, Hunte made a commitment to a new way of life. He solemnly vowed to abide by the movement's tenets of 'complete honesty, purity, love and unselfishness'.

Rarely in the annals of sport can a four-month road trip have had such a profound impact on every aspect of the life of an elite sportsperson.

When he died suddenly in Sydney in December 1999 at the age of 67 the noble game mourned a noble man; a humanitarian, a social reformer and educator, an activist and a special friend to

Left: Sir Conrad Hunte. Humanitarian, social reformer, educator, mentor to the young and the finest opening batsman Garfield Sobers has seen. *Gordon Brooks*

the young. Hunte was given a State funeral in his beloved Barbados, to which he had returned to live earlier that year after 43 years of carrying the standard of Moral Rearmament throughout the world.

He was the second member of the 1960–61 team to die — after captain Frank Worrell in 1967. Just 29 days earlier he had been a pallbearer at the funeral of 41-year-old Malcolm Marshall, perhaps the greatest of all the West Indian fast bowlers and another favourite son of Barbados.

Renowned for the strength of his fight against prejudice, fear, ignorance and intolerance, Hunte served the movement in England, Papua New Guinea, Fiji and, in the last seven years of his life, in the new Republic of South Africa.

Hunte drew his enormous strength from his God and from the teachings of the Indian political and religious leader and pacifist Mahatma Gandhi and during his time in South Africa worked from Johannesburg where Gandhi so famously developed his creed of passive resistance against injustice.

He used his ministry, as the national coach of the United Cricket Board of South Africa, as a vehicle to reach and teach the

Coach and surrogate father. Conrad Hunte with undergraduates of the United Cricket Board of South Africa's development program at Alexandra township, Johannesburg in 1994. *Michael Rayner*

dispossessed and disadvantaged. He was adamant that God's power, not black power, was the answer to white power, and this fervent belief underpinned his personal philosophy. When he reached South Africa in 1992, Hunte declared:

I have been prepared by history and by the commitment of my faith for this moment ... My whole upbringing has been a preparation for this moment.

His widow, Patricia, the mother of their three daughters, was among those who wondered whether it was his destiny to die in Australia. It was as though a circle had been completed, she told friends.

At the time of his death Hunte was in the company of Jim Coulter, a close friend who had introduced him to the Moral Rearmament movement 39 years earlier. On the eve of the fourth Test match in Adelaide in January 1961, Coulter happened to hear a radio talk by Hunte tracing the history of the West Indian people from the days of slavery to the independence of the archipelago. Coulter was deeply moved by the address — Out of Darkness into Light — and felt he had been called to contact Hunte.

It was Coulter who endeavoured to revive Hunte after he suffered a massive heart attack following a game of tennis, just hours before he was scheduled to give the keynote address at the opening of an international conference of the Moral Rearmament movement at Collaroy, a beachside suburb north of Sydney.

The theme of Hunte's speech was 'An agenda of hope for the new millennium'.

The eldest of nine children whose father worked on a sugar plantation at Shorey Village on the east coast of Barbados, Hunte included a reference to his early days in his 'agenda of hope'.

You are looking at someone who before he drew his first breath, before he took his first step, had three strikes against him. I speak in terms of the prejudice some people hold towards people like me. I was born black. I was born poor. I was born disenfranchised. According to a lack of vision of those people, I am not expected to stand where I stand today.

A powerful and witty orator with a high-pitched and infectious laugh, Hunte vigorously and eloquently advanced the cause of racial harmony and understanding. To this end he made a close study of the emotional and psychological problems known to have afflicted high-profile black athletes confronted by prejudice.

It was the response to his 'Out of Darkness into Light' program that compelled Hunte to examine his life and personal philosophy.

I received a lot of letters from all over the country thanking me for enlightening people about the West Indies. They said God must be using me for some remarkable purpose. I thought that if this was so then I had to find a way to change my own private life to match my public performance.

The fates decreed that at the very moment Hunte sought to change his life Coulter succeeded in reaching him and invited him to see the film The Crowning Experience, screening at the Atheneum Theatre in Collins Street, Melbourne.

I saw my own life in that film which was about Mary McLeod Bethune, who was a child of slave parents who became an adviser to American President Roosevelt. Her rise to fame was not enough, and she needed something new in her life. So from that moment I became enamoured and committed to this idea. It is a moral and spiritual commitment to life which means you live by absolute moral values on and off the field, and by silence. As Mahatma Gandhi says: 'The only terror I bow to is the terror of the inner voice.' To listen in silence for direction and correction and to live by these absolute values on and off the field has made a considerable difference to how I live and what I live for. Australia holds a very central part in my own life and make-up because of the encounter I faced in Melbourne in 1960–61. I have a number of homes in the world. One is in Barbados, where I was born; one in England, where I've adopted my second home; one in America, where my wife comes from; and the fourth is in Australia - my spiritual home.

❋ ❋ ❋

Change of season. Conrad Hunte tightens straps on the pad of Philip Beggs at an impromptu coaching session at a Melbourne park in the 1960s. Beggs' friend Joe Thwaites is entrusted with the football.
Jim Coulter

A richly talented opening batsman who was prepared to temper his stroke play to ensure a solid foundation for an innings, Hunte played 44 Tests between 1957–58 and 1966–67, accumulating 3245 runs at 45.06 with eight centuries.

He made his first-class debut in 1950–51, but had to wait seven years to play his first Test series against Pakistan. He announced himself emphatically with 142 on debut in front of his home crowd, and in the third Test in Jamaica scored 260 in a partnership of 446 when Garfield Sobers amassed a then record unbeaten 365.

He returned 662 runs at 77.75 for the series and thereafter was an automatic selection. He was West Indies' vice-captain for eight years, first to Worrell, whom he revered, and then to Sobers.

According to eminent West Indian broadcaster and writer Tony Cozier, Hunte admitted subsequently that he was so deeply hurt when Sobers was appointed captain ahead of him, reportedly on Worrell's advice, that he contemplated quitting. Characteristically, his Christian principles prompted him to ask forgiveness for his initial reaction and he remained, as a stabilising influence as deputy to the often impetuous Sobers.

Frank Misson dives full length forward to spectacularly run out Conrad Hunte off his own bowling during the remarkable Adelaide Test. Rohan Kanhai (running to the non-striker's end) blamed himself for the misjudgment which in all probability cost Hunte his second century of the series.
News Ltd

In his tribute to Hunte, Sobers said:

Some people said Conrad did not support me while I was captain but he was a very good friend to me and supported me 100 per cent in the game and outside of it. It was a pleasure to play with him and I have to say I think he was the greatest opening batsman I have seen.

While he lived outside the Caribbean nearly all his adult life, Hunte's interest in cricket and cricketers never waned, and he closely monitored the health of the game in Barbados and throughout the archipelago.

On a visit to his homeland in 1991 for the 21st anniversary of the Conrad Hunte Sports Club at Shorey Village, he said publicly that he feared the excesses of competitiveness and professionalism in the modern game had tarnished the good name of West Indies cricket. At the time there was widespread criticism of the mentali-

Vale Sir Conrad. Sir Everton Weekes (centre), Wes Hall (left) and Tony King (far right) were among the pallbearers at the State funeral accorded Sir Conrad in his beloved Barbados in December 1999.
Gordon Brooks

September 1960 and Australia bound.
(From left) Rohan Kanhai, Garfield Sobers,
Wes Hall, masseur 'Manny' Alves, Conrad
Hunte and Sonny Ramadhin aboard the liner
Strathaird at Tilbury docks at the start of the
voyage to Fremantle.
Reuters

ty and methodology employed by the West Indies to maintain their supremacy in world cricket:

It does sadden me that some of our top players are beginning to break the spirit of the game. It takes a strong mind and spirit to be able to absorb such high glory that sportsmen and film stars have. There is no point in winning matches and losing the respect of the people.

He was deeply distressed at the decline of West Indies cricket in the second half of the 1990s, and his election to the presidency of the Barbados Cricket Association just before his death was widely interpreted as a move towards a wider involvement in West Indian cricket.

Of all the tributes paid to Hunte, the one from Stephen Alleyne, in his capacity as acting president of the Barbados Cricket Association, had particular resonance.

In a cricket world that seems rent by fractiousness and discord, could it be that Sir Conrad was sent as a symbol of unity and tolerance and the beacon to a brighter tomorrow?

12

A BAIL AND A POLTERGEIST

Fifth Test

Melbourne: 10, 12, 13, 14, 15 February

That such an enthralling Test series ended so controversially was cause for considerable regret. Given the evenness of the teams and their commitment to excellence and entertainment it was perhaps unsurprising that the result of the series came down to this.

In the quest for 258 for victory and a 2–1 series scoreline, Australia, on the fifth day, were 7–254, with wily veterans Alf Valentine and Wally Grout involved in a tense duel. Grout, straining to remain calm, daringly late-cut against Valentine. However, rather than follow the passage of the ball, keeper Gerry Alexander stood over the wicket, immediately drawing attention to the fact the off bail was on the ground.

High controversy. Wicketkeeper Gerry Alexander indicates to umpire Colin Egar (out of picture) that the off bail has been dislodged. Wally Grout, oblivious to the situation, is near to completing the first of two runs. Alf Valentine, the bowler, (bottom left) surveys the scene. *News Ltd*

After two runs were taken, umpire Colin Egar, at the bowler's end, walked to square leg to consult with his colleague Colin Hoy. According to 'Johnnie' Moyes, Hoy later revealed that Grout had not hit the wicket with his bat and that Alexander had not inadvertently dislodged the bail.

Egar said that he had been unsighted and, with Hoy's blessing, gave Grout the benefit of the doubt.

Moyes wrote: 'Most of us felt that he [Egar] might well have taken a little longer to weigh up the possibilities and probabilities. If he had done so he must have inevitably come to the conclusion that Grout was out, benefit of the doubt or no benefit of the doubt. Legally the umpire was thoroughly justified in giving the decision he did, but the circumstantial evidence was all in favour of the bowler.'

The decision riled sections of the crowd of 41,186 and Peter Lashley, at least, sagged to the ground in an overt show of disappointment until reproved by Frank Worrell.

What caused the bail to fall remains a mystery to this day, although Moyes was in no doubt that Grout had played the ball onto his wicket. The bail fell a fraction of a second after the ball passed the stumps and in front of, not behind the wicket.

Moyes claimed Grout made a move as though to walk but Ken Mackay waved him back into his crease. Always renowned for his sportsmanship, Grout then swung lustily at Valentine and was caught in the gully by Cammie Smith. Whether or not he sacrificed his wicket is still debated, more than 30 years after his death. Richie Benaud was certain he did not. Moyes, and some players, Garfield Sobers included, were adamant that he did.

With two runs required and two wickets in hand, Johnny Martin swung ambitiously at Valentine, skying the ball towards mid-on. But luck's a fortune, and Wes Hall, sore and exhausted from his heavy workload throughout the series, did not react quickly enough to make the ground to take the catch. Instead, Martin stole a single.

With the scores tied, Valentine bowled a gem of a delivery to Mackay. So sure was Alexander that the ball had bowled Mackay that he raised his gloves — and Australia triumphed by two wickets on the resultant bye.

It was a cruel irony that the match should finish in such a fashion, given that Alexander had not only kept brilliantly through the series and taken 16 catches but had also headed the batting averages, with 484 runs at a startling 60.50.

Rain throughout Melbourne over the two days leading up to the match persuaded Benaud to send the West Indies in to bat when he won the toss. It was a bold tactic that surprised critics and, according to the Wisden Cricketers' Almanack, 'sent a murmur of surprise around the ground'. The cognoscenti, however, nodded sagely, noting that on the only other times Benaud had so gambled — against England in Melbourne and Pakistan in Dacca — Australia had triumphed.

February 4, 1961 and Neil Harvey (left) and Frank Misson are buoyed by the news that they have passed medical checks in advance of the final Test match in Melbourne. *News Ltd*

While there was bounce and encouraging movement for both Alan Davidson and Frank Misson, they found it difficult to keep their footing, and sawdust was hurried onto the ground.

Conrad Hunte was subdued at the early loss of Smith and again it was left to Rohan Kanhai to provide some impetus for the innings. When Kanhai fell to a splendid reflex catch by Neil Harvey at slip from the back of Grout's right glove, all momentum was lost until Sobers and Lashley joined forces for a fifth wicket partnership of 93.

Whether or not it was a misjudgment by Benaud or simply the vagaries of the pitch, the slow men soon became the greater danger, and Benaud involved Bob Simpson to a much greater extent that at any other time in the series. While Benaud accounted for Lashley, Simpson again confounded Sobers with his googly, and had him neatly caught at the wicket by Grout. There were

Colin McDonald is a study in concentration at practice at the Melbourne Cricket Ground. He was thrilled to score one run a thousand for the then world record crowd of 90,800 who watched the second day's play. *News Ltd*

flashes of brilliance by Sobers, but overall he was restrained and at times unusually uncertain — especially against Simpson. He took 177 minutes over 64; Hunte toiled for 146 minutes for his 31.

By the dizzy standards of the series it was a most unexceptional day — 252 runs coming from 75 overs.

There was some speculation that Benaud's decision to send the West Indies in to bat was based on the belief that Hall, jaded though he was, would be more manageable on a harder, drier and less erratic second-day pitch. Whether or not this was a part of Benaud's reasoning it proved to be the case, and a world record crowd of 90,800 rejoiced in some fine batting by the Australian upper order after Joe Solomon had overseen the West Indies' tailenders, lifting the tally to 292.

With the pitch losing its venom Hall held few fears for Colin McDonald and Simpson, who had to be more alert and watchful against the slow bowlers — especially Lance Gibbs, who was in fine fettle. While Simpson seemed hampered as a result of a crack on the forearm, McDonald played with freedom and confidence, and their stand of 146 was the first century opening partnership of the series. There was a collective groan of disappointment when McDonald was leg before wicket to Sobers just nine short of his century. He had batted for 166 minutes and struck six fours.

The West Indies brightened noticeably when Norm O'Neill and Simpson fell with the score at 181, but at the end of a day which saw the West Indies fielding reach a high standard of excellence, Australia were just 60 in arrears, with seven wickets in hand. Indeed, Moyes contended that aside from the batting of McDonald and Peter Burge, the fielding was the highlight of the day for the vast throng.

An exhausted Hall dug deep early on the third day to remove Mackay, his solitary wicket for the Test match, and when Sobers dismissed the lame Harvey with a wicked lifting delivery, the West Indies sensed that they were back in the contest.

Davidson scored his 1000th Test run while providing some late assistance for the admirably resolute Burge (68 in 194 minutes), but while they finished with a first innings advantage of 64, the Australians had squandered the powerful position given them by McDonald and Simpson.

Indeed, they lost their last seven wickets for 112 as Sobers gave one of his command performances with the ball. Worrell first summoned Sobers with the score at 0–124 half an hour before tea on Saturday, and he did not relieve him until the score was 9–335, on Monday.

On Monday, instead of bowling spin as he had on Saturday, Sobers took the new ball and bowled with sustained hostility. In all he bowled 44 overs for his figures of 5–120. Sobers and Gibbs, who had the imposing figures of 4–74 from 38.4 overs, had to cover for Valentine, who was out of action on Monday having awoken with badly swollen hands. The previous evening at a soirée he had made his debut on the bongo drums!

Hunte and Smith erased 54 of the deficit in just 61 minutes before Davidson, sore after treatment for a wrenched knee, trapped Smith for 37. To the delight of a crowd of 51,391 Smith had played with customary abandon, punctuating his hand with five boundaries and a six flicked over long-on against Misson.

Keen to rest Sobers after his marathon bowling performance, Worrell promoted Solomon when Kanhai thumped a long hop from Benaud straight to Misson at mid-wicket.

Kanhai had been in sparkling touch, and his dismissal was a severe blow to the cause. Nevertheless, the West Indians fought back bravely, and with two days remaining led by 62 runs with eight wickets in hand.

Despite pain from serious injuries, Davidson and Grout again

pooled their resources at the start of the fourth day. Just nine runs had been added when Hunte attempted to drive through the covers but managed only to offer a catch at the wicket.

X-rays had confirmed Grout's suspicion that he'd chipped a bone in his right wrist, and he winced as he completed the dismissal. A tough hand with tough hands, Grout made light of his discomfort and by the end of the day had taken three more catches, to boost the number of his dismissals for the series to 23 — equalling the world record jointly held by Alexander (against England in 1959–60) and South Africa's John Waite (against New Zealand in 1953–54.) His achievement was all the more remarkable given that he did not make a single dismissal in the fourth Test.

Fifteen of his wickets came from the bowling of Davidson. Despite missing the Adelaide Test with injury, Davidson finished with 33 wickets, thus matching the record of Clarrie Grimmett against 'Jackie' Grant's first West Indies team to visit Australia in 1930–31. He claimed five or more wickets in an innings for the fifth time and combined with O'Neill to smartly run out Solomon for 36 as he was threatening to build a substantial and decisive partnership with Alexander.

When Lashley, the last of the recognised batsmen, was trapped leg before wicket by a quicker delivery from Martin, the West Indies were 7–262 and leading by 198 runs. A customary flurry of activity by Hall under the supervision of Alexander, who completed his sixth half-century of the series, saw a final score of 321.

With Australia required to bat for a little over an hour, Benaud went to Simpson with a daring instruction. In effect, he told Simpson to flay Hall, and if the plan failed he would accept full responsibility with Sir Donald Bradman and his fellow selectors.

Brandishing his bat like a cutlass, Simpson dumbfounded the West Indians by tearing four boundaries and a two off Hall's first over. With adrenaline coursing through his veins he took nine runs from Hall's second over — Worrell had no option but to withdraw him after he had conceded 31 runs in three overs. However, Benaud's hopes of getting through to stumps unscathed were dashed when Smith held a brilliant diving catch behind

A pensive Rohan Kanhai emerging from the West Indies dressingroom in the Grey Smith stand at the Melbourne Cricket Ground. Kanhai developed a fondness for the great ground after scoring a superlative 252 against Victoria in advance of the first Test.
Alf Batchelder

point to remove McDonald off Gibbs' sixth delivery.

As though to underscore the fact that he should be held responsible for the radical modus operandi, Benaud emerged as nightwatchman to shepherd Simpson through to stumps. At the close of play Simpson had scored 44, with five boundaries (all off Hall), and Australia, with nine wickets in hand, needed 201 to win.

It was soon apparent to Worrell that the pitch would provide no assistance to Hall, and that he would need to share the bulk of the workload with Gibbs and Valentine if the West Indies were to prevail.

After Benaud played recklessly across the line and was bowled by Valentine, O'Neill joined Simpson. While the going was fraught, especially against Gibbs, they held out until lunch and advanced the total to 2–153.

Immediately after the adjournment the pendulum swung again when Simpson, just eight runs shy of his first Test century, played on to Gibbs. He had been tempted to cut after Worrell removed a slip for Gibbs.

O'Neill seemed burdened by the responsibility he was compelled to accept following Simpson's demise, and played with a lack of certainty. Moments after surviving an emphatic leg before wicket appeal, the indefatigable Worrell had him caught at the wicket two short of his half-century.

Suddenly, the weight of the world was upon the shoulders of Burge, and he met the challenge manfully, especially after Harvey, at last unrestricted in his movements, got a leading edge against a full toss from Worrell and was caught by Smith at extra cover.

A rare error of judgment by Sobers at mid-on enabled Davidson to remain with Burge with the score at 5–208. Had Sobers held the straightforward catch Australia would have been 6–205 and the tension in the Australian rooms would have been even greater.

The persistence, courage and skill of Worrell and Gibbs, his junior by 10 years, was never more evident than in this second session. They bowled unchanged for 39 overs and conceded just 55 runs, dramatically reviving the West Indies' chances.

The much-loved Ken 'Slasher' Mackay proving his fitness at the Albert Ground, Melbourne on the eve of the final Test. He was at the wicket when victory came.
News Ltd

Promptly after tea Burge struck three boundaries — two off Gibbs and one off Worrell — but Davidson edged Worrell, and this time Sobers made no mistake. When Burge played on to Valentine after a quality innings of 53, there was suddenly the possibility of a West Indies victory.

As had been the case in Brisbane and Adelaide, the tension was scarcely bearable.

Had Hall reached a skied offering from Mackay the intensity of feeling may have been even greater, if indeed that were possible. Ironically, the tired and sore Hall and the fast and irrepressible Kanhai had swapped positions only moments before.

It was then, at 7–254, that Valentine turned and bowled to Grout.

ON REFLECTION

LANCE GIBBS: I was at slip at the time and I thought he was bowled. You could hear the click.

ALF VALENTINE: The bail didn't come off: I hit the bail off — he was bowled.

GERRY ALEXANDER: He [Wally Grout] got an inside edge and it also went on to the stumps. And I was standing there looking disappointed and perplexed — perplexed because he hadn't been given out and disappointed because it could have been put down as another dropped catch. It was an inside edge — it hit the inside edge of Wally's bat and hit the stump ever so delicately.

CONRAD HUNTE: Alf Valentine used to spin the ball quite viciously from leg, make it spin for the right-hander. But he also had a very good arm ball that would come into you from the off if you were a right-hander. That's the ball he bowled to Wally. Now the ball is coming into Wally and he is expecting a leg break. He comes down across the ball and therefore hits an inside edge and it hits the side of the wicket. Therefore the bail falls forward. Very unusual; consequently the umpire thinks someone must have touched it because the bail doesn't normally fall forward. Once again — one of those extraordinary things.

PETER LASHLEY: When the bail fell off and the runs were completed and the 'not out' came I fell forward to the ground. I was on my way down when I heard a shout from mid-off, I think Frank Worrell was there, and before I hit the ground I was back up, because I realised I had violated his edict on no demonstrations.

WES HALL: I think if Grout had been given bowled rather than given those two runs I believe we would have won.

BOB SIMPSON: There was a huge crack where the off stump was set. Whether in fact Gerry [Alexander] had trod on that crack ... If you trod on some of those cracks at the old Melbourne Cricket Ground — if you didn't fall down them — you were going to move them. There could have been a bit of movement there.

ALAN DAVIDSON: The amazing part about it is that the bail was in front of the stump. I think it's one of those things that without the modern-day replays I don't think anyone will really know.

GARFIELD SOBERS: Wally just let go one big swing at it and hit it up into the air and he was caught. But that was in the spirit of the way the game was played throughout the whole series. Wally felt there was a kind of discrepancy that nobody seemed to understand. He knew that Gerry Alexander would not have appealed if he had touched the stumps because things had gone so well between the two teams nobody was going to do it. And he felt that there might have been a mistake — the ball might have hit the stumps — and he was batting under false pretences, so he just threw his wicket away.

COLIN McDONALD: That 90,800 turned up that day was the highlight as far as I was concerned, because I made one run a thousand. I enjoyed that. The fact that many people could turn up on one day was an outpouring of acceptance that the cricket up to then had been fantastic.

RICHIE BENAUD: I suspect the West Indies might have been fractionally down because they thought, and I think they were quite right, they should have won the game in Adelaide. They had plenty of scope to win it and couldn't do it. So I did think we were on a bit of a high, and it was something that helped us make that final Test match quite an event.

ALAN DAVIDSON: The fact we had so many people there I think was a reaction what the whole series had created.

NEIL HARVEY: The place was electric. There is no feeling like it.

RICHIE BENAUD: I went to Bob [Simpson] in the second innings, and said I want you to go out there and take Wes apart. If it doesn't work, then I promise you, I'll take the blame for it. But I want you to tear him to bits. And he did. It got us on the way. You have a look at the score card and you'll see precisely what Simmo did. I thought that was very important in the context of the way the game was going.

The Melbourne Cricket Ground is the ground of the people and thousands of spectators race to embrace their heroes at the end of an unforgettable series. *ABC*

13

THE PRIZE

Given his nervousness at the start of the series, Sir Donald Bradman could never have foreseen the wave of emotion that engulfed the Melbourne Cricket Ground on 15 February 1961.

After Mackay and Martin had run the bye which gave Australia a two-wicket victory and so a 2–1 series success, thousands of people ran onto the ground. And that is where they stayed — about 25,000 of the 41,186 who had been absorbed by the final day's play. It was patently clear that they did not want the series to end, and they waited excitedly but patiently to show their respects to Benaud and Worrell and their men.

When these great generals, along with Sir Donald, the board chairman, finally emerged from the Grey Smith Stand and took their places on the rostrum for the presentation ceremony, the roar which greeted them was reminiscent of an Australian football finals crowd.

Named after distinguished Melbourne Cricket Club president Frank Grey Smith, the stand was the forerunner to the western stand (1968), which in turn was renamed the Ponsford stand in 1986, and to this day provides the dressingroom facilities for the game's elite players.

As one extraordinary contest followed another throughout

The Frank Worrell Trophy. *ABC*

the hot summer, Sir Donald thought it would be appropriate to strike a trophy to celebrate the series and all future rubbers between the teams.

His belief that the trophy should be named in honour of Worrell was accepted enthusiastically by the board and by Benaud and the Australian players.

Benaud recalls: I suppose it would have been around Adelaide (fourth Test), I'm not absolutely certain, when Sir Donald came to me and said they were going to produce a trophy which Ernie McCormick was going to do and it would be called the Frank Worrell Trophy. He was the driving force. It was his idea. I said: 'That's absolutely wonderful.' And that's how it came about. It was a lovely ceremony, and it was very nice to be the first one to receive the Frank Worrell Trophy.

McCormick, who opened the attack for Australia in 12 Tests in the 1930s, was a prominent jeweller in Melbourne.

Mercifully, he filed his design and sketches et al in a safe place — they were required in 1991, before his death at the age of 85, when it was discovered that the famous trophy was missing and a replica would have to be crafted.

To the acute embarrassment of Wes Hall, the original trophy was discovered when he was sorting through his mother Iona's possessions after her death in Barbados in January 1994.

A decade earlier, Hall had managed Clive Lloyd's barnstorming farewell tour of Australia which the West Indies won 3–1. To ensure that the trophy was safe, Hall placed it with some personal items to be taken back to Barbados by his assistant manager, Cammie Smith, while he remained with the West Indies team at the World Championship of Cricket in Melbourne early in 1985.

As it happened, the trophy was very safe, but the fact that no one knew its whereabouts caused considerable awkwardness among administrators for some time.

In February 1961 the trophy, featuring a ball from the tied Test match, gleamed in its pristine beauty as it was presented to the Australian people for the first time.

Michael Charlton, the noted broadcaster with a voice like liquid chocolate, acted as master of ceremonies and introduced Sir Donald Bradman.

Sir Donald Bradman: Ladies and gentlemen, I'm very sad to say that the time has come to ring down the curtain on this series of Test matches.

But I speak to you today as chairman of the Australian Board of Control for International Cricket, and on our own behalf and on behalf of the cricket-loving public of Australia, I want to pay tribute to the captains and the two teams who have provided us with such magnificent cricket this summer. (Sustained applause)

You've all heard so much about the great revival that has taken place in cricket, and for that we thank our West Indian guests who have come here (Loud applause), and they have made it possible and they have given us some superb cricket.

Live cross. Distinguished broadcaster Michael Charlton interviewing the captains after Frank Worrell had formally presented the prize to Richie Benaud. *Alf Batchelder*

But I would also like to say that I think Richie and his boys have been equally responsible and have played their full part.

Now as you know, we had a tie in Brisbane — the most fantastic finish in history — and in order to commemorate that wonderful occasion the Board of Control created a trophy for permanent competition between Australia and the West Indies. (Applause)

And it was decided, in honour of a very brilliant cricketer who unfortunately has now played his last Test match in Australia, that we should call it the Frank Worrell Trophy. (Sustained applause)

As you know, ladies and gentlemen, Frank Worrell has been, and in fact still is, a great cricketer in the artistic mould, and there aren't very many of them about, and we regret deeply that we shan't have the pleasure of seeing him again. But in addition, I can tell you he's a grand sportsman and he's a very gallant loser. (Applause)

This trophy which we have here, I'm going to hand it to Frank, and I'm going to ask him to present it to Richie, who is the winning captain, and the next time these two teams meet, which will probably be in the West Indies, then they will play again for this trophy.

You'll find that it has on the top of it one of the cricket balls used in the famous tied match in Brisbane. (Applause)

And there is the trophy, ladies and gentlemen ... and I know these boys are very tired, because they've had a very trying match, so without further ado I will hand this over to Frank, thank him once again for the wonderful performance they've put up this year and ask him to do the honours ... (Sustained applause)

Worrell uttered only, 'Mr Chairman ...' before he was drowned out by a spontaneous and emotional rendition of 'For he's a jolly good fellow ...'.

And on a cue of 'hip, hip' from the strident and unmistakably Australian voice that had led the singing, three cheers for Worrell resounded around the great stadium.

After further applause, Worrell composed himself and resumed.

Frank Worrell: Thank you ladies and gentlemen. This is indeed a very sad and happy occasion, because the drawing of the stumps this afternoon marked the end of the most sensational, interesting and enjoyable series that any West Indies team has ever been engaged in. It also marks the culmination of a very enjoyable stay in your country, and we would like to thank all those people for their very kindly letters and all of you for the lavish hospitality. We are also sad to think that we shan't be taking this back with us. (Laughter) Judging from the standard of the batting today, well, I think I'm left with the duty of explaining to our people at home what this trophy looks like, what it feels like (Laughter), and I shall be able to tell them where it is (Laughter) and where it is likely to stay until we meet you again. (Sustained applause)

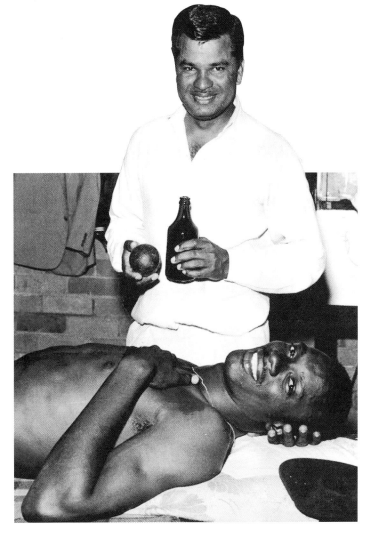

In all likelihood a recumbent Wes Hall is far more interested in the bottle than the ball that Sonny Ramadhin has on offer. Hall demonstrated extraordinary courage and resilience to spearhead the West Indies attack through such a long and demanding campaign.
News Ltd

We've had a very enjoyable tour, and if fortune decrees that this trophy should stay in Australia, we have got to congratulate Richie and his men for their wonderful fight back in Adelaide and for dominating the scene here in this match. And we are looking forward to seeing this trophy in the West Indies, where we shall try to wrest it from you in the same friendly and exciting manner as it has been won during this series. (Applause)

I've got two duties to perform. I've got to present this trophy to Richie and congratulate him and his men for the wonderful cricket.

Secondly, I've got a little token which I would like to present to him also ...

Firstly, Richie, congratulations to you and the boys. (Applause)

And finally, ladies and gentlemen, we've got a symbol here of a scalp (cap). (Uproarious applause)

Secondly, you can have my neck (tie). (Applause and laughter)

And you can have the upper half of my body (blazer). (Sustained applause)

I shall refrain from offering the lower half of my body because the knees wouldn't stand him in any stead.

Thank you all.

Richie Benaud: Sir Donald Bradman, Frank, ladies and gentlemen, Frank was kind enough to say that he was offering me a scalp, and his neck and the upper half of his body, but I'm quite certain that you will all agree with me that he himself will remain in the hearts of cricket lovers in this country for many a long day. (Sustained applause)

It's always a very sad thing to come to the end of a Test series, it's always a very happy thing to have won, and in this particular instance, it is a magnificent moment to stand here in front of all you people and to be able to stay that having played in this my fiftieth Test match, I've never played in five more memorable nor more enjoyable games. Nor have I and my team ever played against a finer bunch of cricketers than these West Indians.

The trophy that has been so well named, the Frank Worrell Trophy, was the finish of an idea that started after that memorable Brisbane Test. And I put it to you that the Australian Board of Control could have chosen no finer name for that trophy than the one they eventually came up with. For I've come to know Frank pretty well in this particular season — you generally get to know your opposing team and your opposing captain pretty well — and I would like to tell you that it has not only been a pleasure to play against our visitors and against Frank but to play in a series as captain opposite Frank Worrell has been a privilege. (Applause)

I'm terribly sorry that this particular Test match marks the end of Frank's Test career (in Australia), but it is quite obvious from this trophy that has been perpetuated in his name for competition between the countries that he will certainly not be forgotten, and I'm sure I can speak for the cricket-loving public of Australia who've enjoyed these matches so much that I say, Frank, that everyone wants you to come back here again — if you don't come back as a player then do as Gerry Gomez did and come back as a manager — and I do hope that when that occasion arises the 90,000 crowd that you saw here the other day will be exceeded. (Applause)

There is little more I can say except thank you to all you people out here who have supported the game and supported cricket this year, and a very, very big thank you to my own team who gave me such wonderful support during the series, and an even bigger thank you to our West Indian friends and Frank, who have done such a wonderful job. Thank you. (Sustained applause)

Sir Donald Bradman: Ladies and gentlemen, that concludes our little ceremony. And I think now everybody can go home and save up their pennies for the next series. Thank you very much.

And with that, and to the strains of Waltzing Matilda being piped through the public address system, a Test series that had been full of exceptional cricket and exceptional goodwill ended.

ON REFLECTION

CONRAD HUNTE: It was a fitting tribute to a man whose leadership made an impact on West Indies and world cricket. The trophy bears forever the memory of someone who gave greatly to the game of cricket.

GARFIELD SOBERS: The two captains set their sights on a tremendous series and their hopes were fulfilled, and they expressed their feelings and sentiments at the end of the series by exchanging things. It was very touching. The Frank Worrell Trophy will always be there, and will always bring back memories of him and the tour of 1960–61.

WES HALL: The Frank Worrell Trophy wasn't a reality at the beginning of the tour. I think it was conceptualised because of the cricket played between the two teams, the camaraderie between the two teams and the people's appreciation of the type of cricket that was played. It was a symbol of excellence.

ALAN DAVIDSON: There wasn't an Australian player who disagreed with it being [called] the Frank Worrell Trophy. We accepted that as the tribute for what was an incredible series. There was a lot of give, there was a lot of take, but at the end of the day it could never be emulated. It set the standard for what you should look for in cricket.

CAMMIE SMITH: We could all feel a sense of pride that the Australians could name it the Frank Worrell Trophy. That spoke volumes, and it told us the high esteem in which he was held.

BOB SIMPSON: We thought the naming of the trophy was a fitting reward, and it was accepted in that spirit.

ALF VALENTINE: To have this trophy named after Sir Frank Worrell - well he wasn't Sir Frank then, just Frank Worrell — was a great accomplishment for Worrell and for West Indies cricket. I mean, having the first black captain. We were waiting a long time for something like this to happen.

ROHAN KANHAI: When you think about a foreign captain getting beaten in the series and naming a trophy after him, to be handing over [that trophy] to the winning captain ... For us it was an achievement we never thought possible. But it was. And we were proud of it.

14

Under the Gaze of the Knight

The egalitarianism of Australian cricket had never been more evident. And it gladdened the hearts of the West Indians. Only Frank Worrell and his now senior professionals Alf Valentine and Sonny Ramadhin had toured nine years earlier and experienced the unpretentiousness of Australian cricket culture and the accessibility of the game's luminaries.

That they could even become acquainted with Sir Donald Bradman is an abiding memory of the tour for many in the party.

The beginning of the 1960s was a seminal period in Sir Donald's career as administrator nonpareil, and on 13 September, six weeks before the West Indies started their tour at Bunbury, Western Australia, he was elected unopposed for his first three-year term as chairman of the board.

It was, however, as the chairman — a least nominally — of the Australian selection panel that the West Indian players came to know Sir Donald. (Phil Ridings, his successor as a selector in

Sir Donald Bradman: The most influential cricket person of the 20th century. *ABC*

The last word. (From left) Selectors Dudley Seddon, Sir Donald Bradman and Jack Ryder. *Age*

February 1971, was the first official chairman when entrusted to lead the panel in choosing the 1977 team for England).

Throughout the summer it was not uncommon for Sir Donald to leave his fellow selectors, Jack Ryder and Dudley Seddon, and sit and chat with either the Australian or West Indies players. Or, as was the case in Brisbane on the patio outside the dressingroom, with players of both at the one time.

While he was new to the duties of chairman, he had served as a South Australian delegate to the board since 1945 and, at the age of 52, had already established a reputation as a formidable administrator.

He took an intense interest in this series not simply because it was his duty as board chairman to do so but because he believed fervently that Richie Benaud and Worrell led teams that were both capable of playing with an attractiveness and excitement that could reignite public interest in Test match cricket.

With the exception of a brief period in 1952–53 when his son, John, was battling serious illness, Sir Donald had been a selector since 1936–37, and he considered these captains and their subordinates manna from heaven at such a sensitive time in the evolution of the game. It was a challenging time, when the game was being blighted everywhere by England's unimaginative, uninspired Test cricket and festering controversies surrounding, throwing, dragging and short-pitched bowling.

Earlier in 1960 the Australian board members had registered their concern at the game's impending crisis by sending their then chairman, Bill Dowling and Sir Donald to London for the annual meeting of the Imperial Cricket Conference (now International Cricket Council.) Traditionally, proxies living in England had represented Australia.

Irving Rosenwater's definitive 1978 biography of Bradman refers to Sir Donald's trepidation when he returned to Australia in August in advance of his election to the chairmanship.

If the throwing controversy was not contained it could lead 'to the greatest catastrophe in cricket history', Sir Donald was reported as saying. 'It is the most complex problem I have known in cricket,' he added, as the international cricket community sought a uniform definition of 'throwing'.

While Sir Donald may not have burdened the young protagonists with his apprehensions, the Australians, at least, gauged the extent of his concern when he so famously addressed them before the first Test in Brisbane.

Alan Davidson recalls: From about 1958, when we played England in Australia Sir Donald really took a personal interest in the whole of the team. He would join us sometimes, by invitation, for our dinners the night before a game. His influence, I think, was about us trying to play attractive cricket.

Neil Harvey, who began his illustrious career under Sir Donald in Australia and England in 1948 and was later to serve with him as a national selector, was fascinated by the relationship between Sir Donald and Benaud:

The players were aware of the rapport between Richie and Don. I think it was probably as close a rapport as I've seen between the chairman of selectors and the captain. They've always got on very well. I think they still do. During the

Neil Harvey cuts late and delicately during the third Test in Sydney. *News Ltd*

time I was involved as vice-captain to Richie and Don was the boss of the selectors they were very close. They always talked about the way the game should be played and not necessarily about individual players.

Simpson, who was destined to succeed Benaud as captain three seasons later, has long recognised he benefited greatly from the guidance quietly offered by Sir Donald:

Sir Donald was wonderful to me. He was always helpful. He was the sort of person who was about but he didn't push his views unless you sought them out. He would always come into the dressingroom at lunchtime or at afternoon tea and be there for the captain or any of the players if they wanted to chat to him. Apart from that he was generally up in the grandstand. But he was available, and I found, particularly when I was captain, that he was an enormous help to me. And always accessible, even today.

With the help of manager Gerry Gomez, who had toured as a player in 1951–52, and his assistant, Max Marshall, Sir Donald also took a close interest in the welfare of the West Indians, and would encourage and congratulate them as willingly as he would the Australians.

As the greatest accumulator of massive scores in Test cricket — 10 double hundreds and two triple centuries — he was particularly keen to follow the fortunes of Garfield Sobers who two and a half years earlier, at the age of 21, had recorded the highest score in Test cricket: an undefeated 365 against Pakistan at Sabina Park, Kingston.

Sir Donald was also 21 when he scored 334 against England at Headingley, Leeds in July 1930.

Sobers recalls with affection his first meeting with Sir Donald:

I remember playing against New South Wales in Sydney and Richie got me out twice and there were a lot of people saying I couldn't pick Richie; couldn't pick his google. I remember sitting on a little table that they used to have outside the player's dressingroom in the viewing room, and I saw Sir Donald for the first time. I must have looked a bit tense, because I remember him coming over to me, putting his hand on my head and saying: 'Don't you worry, son. You'll get them at the right time.' And when I went to play at the 'Gabba I remember he came and had a word before I went out and when I went out I started to play shots and everything came right.

I remember Richie waltzed right up and bowled me a google which he thought I hadn't picked and as I started to go forward Richie started to put his hands in the air. I came on to the back foot and I hit it past Richie. He just managed to get out of the way and it hit the fence and rebounded. I remember after that innings Sir Donald said it was one of the best innings he's ever seen in Australia. He met me as I was coming off and said: 'Oh, it was a good thing you couldn't pick Richie!'

At the age of 30 Valentine did not have the inhibitions of some of his younger colleagues, and he unselfconsciously sat with Sir Donald on occasions.

An inveterate autograph collector, Valentine often sought the wise counsel as well as the signature of notable cricketers. In England 10 years earlier he had the joy of meeting the great West Indian all-rounder Learie Constantine (later Baron Constantine

Sir Donald and the late Lady Jessie Bradman in the backyard of their home at Kensington Park, South Australia in 1994.
Michael Rayner

of Maraval in Trinidad and Tobago and of Nelson in the County Palatine of Lancaster). That English summer he also sat with the incomparable English all-rounder Wilfred Rhodes — and just listened.

Now approaching the age that Rhodes was in 1950, Valentine's eyes still sparkle as he recalls getting the autograph of both Sir Donald and Lady Jessie Bradman:

I had my little autograph book and I had a page for Sir Donald on one side and I wanted his wife on the other side. I got his but Lady Bradman had gone for something. I was in the dressingroom and he came and got the book from me and took it to his wife, got it autographed and brought it back. The other guys couldn't believe it. They couldn't believe that one of the world's greatest batsmen had the time to come up to a little guy from Jamaica and go and get an autograph. You know, I mean it was something else.

Lance Gibbs, Valentine's spin partner in the last three Tests, remains convinced that Sir Donald was as responsible as the team masseur for ensuring that he regained sufficient fitness to replace Ramadhin, who was out of touch and out of sorts — and, as it turned out, at the end of his 43-match Test career:

Sir Donald had said off-spinners are not very successful in Australia and there was no point in keeping Gibbs here. I heard that and immediately I got fit!

On the penultimate evening of the fourth Test, as Gibbs basked in the glory of taking the first hat-trick in Australia-West Indies cricket, Sir Donald invited Gerry Alexander and Jackie Hendriks to his Kensington Park, Adelaide home for dinner. For the keepers it was a moment to treasure.

Jackie Hendriks: One of my abiding pleasures of the whole tour was being so close to Sir Donald Bradman and hearing him talk about the cricket and analyse it. It had a great effect on me.

Gerry Alexander: One of the delightful experiences of our tour, [for] Jackie Hendriks and myself, was to be invited to Sir Donald's home for dinner. At the end, when we were leaving, we turned to the Don and said: 'Well, it looks as though we've got you tomorrow, Sir Donald.' And he looked at us and said: 'Yes, well it looks that way but if ever there was an occasion for Mackay, it's tomorrow.'

The Don had the last word. Again.

The tie tack commissioned by Sir Donald Bradman and presented to the players and umpires in the tied Test match at Brisbane.
Alan Davidson

FIRST TEST   BRISBANE CRICKET GROUND ('GABBA)

MATCH TIED.   Toss: West Indies

	Day	Close of play	Not out batsmen	Day runs	Day wkts	Day ov.	Day mins	Crowd
9-Dec-60	1	West Indies 7/359	Alexander 21, Ramadhin 9	359	7	84	361	10,678
10-Dec-60	2	West Indies 453, Australia 3/196	O'Neill 28, Favell 1	290	6	75.6	349	15,095
12-Dec-60	3	Australia 505, West Indies 0/0	Hunte 0, Smith 0	309	7	71.3	313	8,050
13-Dec-60	4	West Indies 9/259	Hall 0, Valentine 0	259	9	87.6	364	7,550
14-Dec-60	5	West Indies 284, Australia 232		257	11	72.5	350	4,100
			TOTALS	**1474**	**40**	**391**	**1737**	**45,473**

WEST INDIES 1st Innings

Test #			Runs	Mins	4s,6s		Fall of Wickets				
17	CC Hunte	c Benaud b Davidson	24	37	4,-		Wkt	fow	Runs	Mins	
1	CW Smith	c Grout b Davidson	7	26	0,-		1	23	23	26	Smith / Hunte
24	RB Kanhai	c Grout b Davidson	15	32	3,-		2	42	19	11	Hunte / Kanhai
33	GStA Sobers	c Kline b Meckiff	132	174	21,-		3	65	23	22	Kanhai / Sobers
37,c1	FMM Worrell	c Grout b Davidson	65	159	8,-		4	239	174	153	Sobers / Worrell
10	JS Solomon	hit wicket b Simpson	65	141	8,-		5	243	4	7	Worrell / Solomon
1	PD Lashley	c Grout b Kline	19	36	2,1		6	283	40	38	Lashley / Solomon
21,w	FCM Alexander	c Davidson b Kline	60	190	5,-		7	347	64	98	Solomon / Alexander
42	S Ramadhin	c Harvey b Davidson	12	12	2,-		8	366	19	14	Ramadhin / Alexander
14	WW Hall	st Grout b Kline	50	69	8,-		9	452	86	76	Hall / Alexander
30	AL Valentine	not out	0	2	0,-		10	453	1	2	Alexander / Valentine
	Extras	b 0, lb 3, nb 1, w 0	4								
	Total	**100.6 overs All out**	**453**	**445**	**61,1**						

	Wkts	Runs	Ov	Mdns	nb,w	6s
AK Davidson	5	135	30	2	-,-	-
I Meckiff	1	129	18	0	-,1	1
KD Mackay	0	15	3	0	-,-	-
R Benaud	0	93	24	3	-,-	-
RB Simpson	1	25	8	0	-,-	-
LF Kline	3	52	17.6	6	-,-	-

12th Men: JW Martin (Aus), LR Gibbs (WI)
Umpires: CJ Egar, C Hoy

AUSTRALIA 1st Innings

Test #			Runs	Mins	4s,6s		Fall of Wickets				
40	CC McDonald	c Hunte b Sobers	57	111	6,-		Wkt	fow	Runs	Mins	
7	RB Simpson	b Ramadhin	92	260	7,-		1	84	84	111	McDonald / Simpson
66	RN Harvey	b Valentine	15	63	0,-		2	138	54	64	Harvey / Simpson
14	NC O'Neill	c Valentine b Hall	181	401	22,-		3	194	56	85	Simpson / O'Neill
16	LE Favell	run out	45	93	1,2		4	278	84	94	Favell / O'Neill
25	KD Mackay	b Sobers	35	104	4,-		5	381	103	105	Mackay / O'Neill
31	AK Davidson	c Alexander b Hall	44	81	4,-		6	469	88	83	Davidson / O'Neill
46,c18	R Benaud	lbw b Hall	10	17	0,-		7	484	15	19	Benaud / O'Neill
18,w	ATW Grout	lbw b Hall	4	4	1,-		8	489	5	6	Grout / O'Neill
16	I Meckiff	run out	4	6	0,-		9	496	7	9	Meckiff / O'Neill
12	LF Kline	not out	3	5	0,-		10	505	9	5	O'Neill / Kline
	Extras	b 2, lb 8, nb 1, w 4	15								
	Total	**130.3 overs All out**	**505**	**577**	**45,2**						

	Wkts	Runs	Ov	Mdns	nb,w	6s
WW Hall	4	140	29.3	1	2,-	-
FMM Worrell	0	93	30	0	-,1	-
GStA Sobers	2	115	32	0	2,-	-
AL Valentine	1	82	24	6	-,-	2
S Ramadhin	1	60	15	1	-,-	-

WEST INDIES 2nd Innings

		Runs	Mins	4s,6s	Match Runs		Fall of Wickets				
							Wkt	fow	Runs	Mins	
CC Hunte	c Simpson b Mackay	39	88	5,-	63		1	13	13	22	Smith / Hunte
CW Smith	c O'Neill b Davidson	6	22	0,-	13		2	88	75	66	Hunte / Kanhai
RB Kanhai	c Grout b Davidson	54	112	7,-	69		3	114	26	29	Sobers / Kanhai
GStA Sobers	b Davidson	14	28	2,-	146		4	127	13	18	Kanhai / Worrell
FMM Worrell	c Grout b Davidson	65	151	8,-	130		5	210	83	134	Worrell / Solomon
JS Solomon	lbw b Simpson4	7	222	2,-	112		6	210	0	4	Lashley / Solomon
PD Lashley	b Davidson	0	2	0,-	19		7	241	31	69	Alexander / Solomon
FCM Alexander	b Benaud	5	67	0,-	65		8	250	9	13	Ramadhin / Solomon
S Ramadhin	c Harvey b Simpson	6	11	1,-	18		9	253	3	5	Solomon / Hall
WW Hall	b Davidson	18	11	1,-	68		10	284	31	41	Hall / Valentine
AL Valentine	not out	7	41	0,-	7						
Extras	b 14, lb 7, nb 2, w 0	23			27						
Total	**92.6 overs All out**	**284**	**401**	**26,0**	**737**						

	Wkts	Runs	Ov	Mdns	nb,w	6s	Match
AK Davidson	6	87	24.6	4	-,-	-	11/222
I Meckiff	0	19	4	1	-,-	-	1/148
R Benaud	1	69	31	6	-,1	-	1/162
KD Mackay	1	52	21	7	-,1	-	1/67
LF Kline	0	14	4	0	-,-	-	3/66
RB Simpson	2	18	7	2	-,-	-	3/43
NC O'Neill	0	2	1	0	-,-	-	0/2

AUSTRALIA 2nd Innings

		Runs	Mins	4s,6s	Match Runs		Fall of Wickets				
							Wkt	fow	Runs	Mins	
CC McDonald	b Worrell	16	91	0,-	73		1	1	1	14	Simpson / McDonald
RB Simpson	c sub (LR Gibbs) b Hall	0	14	0,-	92		2	7	6	11	Harvey / McDonald
RN Harvey	c Sobers b Hall	5	10	1,-	20		3	49	42	62	O'Neill / McDonald
NC O'Neill	c Alexander b Hall	26	61	4,-	207		4	49	0	4	McDonald / Favell
LE Favell	c Solomon b Hall	7	20	1,-	52		5	57	8	18	Favell / Mackay
KD Mackay	b Ramadhin	28	78	2,-	63		6	92	35	62	Mackay / Davidson
AK Davidson	run out	80	194	8,-	124		7	226	134	134	Davidson / Benaud
R Benaud	c Alexander b Hall	52	136	6,-	62		8	228	2	4	Benaud / Grout
ATW Grout	run out	2	8	0,-	6		9	232	4	9	Grout / Meckiff
I Meckiff	run out	2	7	0,-	6		10	232	0	1	Meckiff / Kline
LF Kline		0	1	0,-	3						
Extras	b 2, lb 9, nb 0, w 3	14			29						
Total	**68.7 overs All out**	**232**	**314**	**22,0**	**737**						

	Wkts	Runs	Ov	Mdns	nb,w	6s	Match
WW Hall	5	63	17.7	3	2,-	-	9/203
FMM Worrell	1	41	16	3	-,-	-	1/134
GStA Sobers	0	30	8	0	1,-	-	2/145
AL Valentine	0	27	10	4	-,-	-	1/109
S Ramadhin	1	57	17	3	-,-	-	2/117

SECOND TEST   MELBOURNE CRICKET GROUND

AUSTRALIA WON BY SEVEN WICKETS.   Toss: Australia

	Day	Close of play	Not out batsmen	Day runs	Day wkts	Day ov.	Day mins	Crowd
30-Dec-60	1	Australia 348, West Indies 1/1	Hunte 1	349	11	67	346	32,422
31-Dec-60	2	West Indies 2/108	Nurse 35, Kanhai 70	107	1	32.3	150	38,439
2-Jan-61	3	West Indies 181, West Indies 5/129	Hunte 74, Alexander 19	202	13	80	344	65,372
3-Jan-61	4	West Indies 233, Australia 3/70		174	8	55	278	14,032
			TOTALS	832	33	234	1118	150,265

AUSTRALIA 1st Innings

Test #			Runs	Mins	4s,6s	Fall of Wickets				
41	CC McDonald	c Watson b Hall	15	45	1,-	Wkt	fow	Runs	Mins	
8	RB Simpson	c Alexander b Hall	49	103	4,-	1	35	35	45	McDonald / Simpson
67	RN Harvey	c Sobers b Worrell	12	27	2,-	2	60	25	28	Harvey / Simpson
15	NC O'Neill	c Sobers b Worrell	40	90	3,-	3	105	45	30	Simpson / O'Neill
17	LE Favell	c Nurse b Sobers	51	102	5,-	4	155	50	61	O'Neill / Favell
26	KD Mackay	b Ramadhin	74	172	4,-	5	189	34	42	Favell / Mackay
32	AK Davidson	b Hall	35	39	4,1	6	242	53	40	Davidson / Mackay
47,c19	R Benaud	b Hall	2	3	0,-	7	244	2	4	Benaud / Mackay
19,w	ATW Grout	b Watson	5	6	0,-	8	251	7	7	Grout / Mackay
2	JW Martin	b Valentine	55	82	4,1	9	348	97	83	Mackay / Martin
1	FM Misson	not out	0	4	0,-	10	348	0	4	Martin / Misson
	Extras	b 0, lb 7, nb 2, w 1	10							
	Total	66.1 overs All out	348	345	27,2					

	Wkts		Runs	Ov	Mdns	nb,w	6s
WW Hall	4		51	12	2	2,1	-
CD Watson	1		73	12	1	-,-	-
GStA Sobers	1		88	17	1	-,-	-
FMM Worrell	2		50	9	0	-,-	1
AL Valentine	1		55	11.1	1	-,-	1
S Ramadhin	1		21	5	0	-,-	-

12th Men: LF Kline (Aus), CW Smith (WI)

Umpires: CJ Egar, C Hoy

WEST INDIES 1st Innings

Test #			Runs	Mins	4s,6s	Fall of Wickets				
18	CC Hunte	c Simpson b Misson	1	8	0,-	Wkt	fow	Runs	Mins	
11	JS Solomon	c Grout b Davidson	0	5	0,-	1	1	1	5	Solomon / Hunte
2	SM Nurse	c Grout b Davidson	70	305	1,-	2	1	0	3	Hunte / Nurse
25	RB Kanhai	c Harvey b Davidson	84	164	13,-	3	124	123	165	Kanhai / Nurse
34	GStA Sobers	c Simpson b Benaud	9	40	0,-	4	139	15	41	Sobers / Nurse
38,c2	FMM Worrell	b Misson	0	14	0,-	5	142	3	15	Worrell / Nurse
22,w	FCM Alexander	c Favell b Davidson	5	34	0,-	6	160	18	35	Alexander / Nurse
43	S Ramadhin	b Davidson	0	7	0,-	7	160	0	8	Ramadhin / Nurse
15	WW Hall	b Davidson	5	13	0,-	8	166	6	14	Hall / Nurse
6	CD Watson	c McDonald b Benaud	4	27	0,-	9	177	11	27	Nurse / Watson
31	AL Valentine	not out	1	6	0,-	10	181	4	6	Watson / Valentine
	Extras	b 0, lb 0, nb 2, w 0	2							
	Total	69.2 overs All out	181	317	14,0					

	Wkts		Runs	Ov	Mdns	nb,w	6s
AK Davidson	6		53	22	4	-,-	-
FM Misson	2		36	11	0	2,-	-
R Benaud	2		58	27.2	10	-,-	-
JW Martin	0		32	8	1	-,-	-
RB Simpson	0		0	1	1	-,-	-

WEST INDIES 2ND INNINGS (FOLLOW-ON)

		Runs	Mins	4s,6s	Match Runs	Fall of Wickets				
						Wkt	fow	Runs	Mins	
CC Hunte	c Grout b O'Neill	110	270	9,-	111	1	40	40	69	Solomon / Hunte
JS Solomon	hit wicket b Benaud	4	69	0,-	4	2	51	11	16	Nurse / Hunte
SM Nurse	run out	3	15	0,-	73	3	97	46	51	Kanhai / Hunte
RB Kanhai	c Misson b Martin	25	50	3,-	109	4	99	2	10	Sobers / Hunte
GStA Sobers	c Simpson b Martin	0	9	0,-	9	5	99	0	3	Worrell / Hunte
FMM Worrell	c Simpson b Martin	0	2	0,-	0	6	186	87	121	Hunte / Alexander
FCM Alexander	c Grout b Davidson	72	194	7,-	77	7	193	7	9	Ramadhin / Alexander
S Ramadhin	st Grout b Benaud	3	8	0,-	3	8	206	13	27	Hall / Alexander
WW Hall	b Davidson	4	26	0,-	9	9	222	16	25	Watson / Alexander
CD Watson	run out	5	18	0,-	9	10	233	11	14	Alexander / Valentine
AL Valentine	not out	0	14	0,-	1					
Extras	b 2, lb 2, nb 2, w 1	7			9					
Total	**80.4 overs All out**	**233**	**343**	**19,0**	**214**					

	Wkts	Runs	Ov	Mdns	nb,w	6s	Match	
AK Davidson	2	51	15.4	2	-,1	-	8/104	
FM Misson	0	36	12	3	2,-	-	2/72	
R Benaud	2	49	20	3	-,-	-	2/104	
JW Martin	3	56	20	3	-,-	-	3/88	
RB Simpson	0	24	8	0	-,-	-	0/24	
NC O'Neill	1	10	5	1	-,-	-	1/10	

AUSTRALIA 2nd Innings

		Runs	Mins	4s,6s	Match Runs	Fall of Wickets				
						Wkt	fow	Runs	Mins	Out / not out
CC McDonald	c Sobers b Hall	13	39	1,-	28	1	27	27	39	McDonald / Simpson
RB Simpson	not out	27	112	1,-	76	2	27	0	3	Harvey / Simpson
RN Harvey	c Alexander b Hall	0	2	0,-	12	3	30	3	8	O'Neill / Simpson
NC O'Neill	lbw b Watson	0	7	0,-	40	4	0	40*	61	Favell / Simpson
LE Favell	not out	24	60	1,-	75					
Extras	b 4, lb 1, nb 1, w 0	6			16					
Total	**18.4 overs 3 wkts**	**70**	**112**	**3,0**	**418**					

	Wkts	Runs	Ov	Mdns	nb,w	6s	Match	
WW Hall	2	32	9.4	0	1,-	-	6/83	
CD Watson	1	32	9	1	-,-	-	2/105	

THIRD TEST — SYDNEY CRICKET GROUND.

WEST INDIES WON BY 222 RUNS.   Toss: West Indies

	Day	Close of play	Not out batsmen	Day runs	Day wkts	Day ov.	Day mins	Crowd
13-Jan-61	1	West Indies 5/303	Sobers 152, Solomon 4	303	5	69	308	37,198
14-Jan-61	2	West Indies 339, Australia 5/172	Mackay 27, Davidson 3	208	10	67	291	44,331
16-Jan-61	3	Australia 202, West Indies 7/179	Alexander 11, Gibbs 4	209	12	81	318	27,583
17-Jan-61	4	West Indies 326, Australia 2/182	Harvey 84, O'Neill 53	329	5	88	355	26,605
18-Jan-61	5	Australia 241		59	8	25	97	16,493
		TOTALS		**1108**	**40**	**330**	**1369**	**152,210**

WEST INDIES 1st Innings

Test #			Runs	Mins	4s,6s		Fall of Wickets				
19	CC Hunte	c Simpson b Meckiff	34	73	3,-		Wkt	fow	Runs	Mins	
2	CW Smith	c Simpson b Davidson	16	35	3,-		1	48	48	35	Smith / Hunte
26	RB Kanhai	c Grout b Davidson	21	69	2,-		2	68	20	38	Hunte / Kanhai
35	GStA Sobers	c Davidson b Davidson	168	270	25,1		3	89	21	32	Kanhai / Sobers
39,c3	FMM Worrell	c Davidson b Benaud	22	66	4,-		4	152	63	67	Worrell / Sobers
3	SM Nurse	c Simpson b Benaud	43	112	5,-		5	280	128	113	Nurse / Sobers
12	JS Solomon	c Simpson b Benaud	14	57	3,-		6	329	49	58	Solomon / Sobers
23,w	FCM Alexander	c Harvey b Benaud	0	11	0,-		7	329	0	1	Sobers / Alexander
9	LR Gibbs	c Grout b Davidson	0	3	0,-		8	329	0	4	Gibbs / Alexander
16	WW Hall	c Grout b Davidson	10	17	2,-		9	329	0	9	Alexander / Hall
32	AL Valentine	not out	0	15	0,-		10	339	10	15	Hall / Valentine
	Extras	b 6, lb 4, nb 0, w 1	11								
	Total	**81.6 overs All out**	**339**	**369**	**47,0**						

	Wkts	Runs	Ov	Mdns	nb,w	6s
AK Davidson	5	80	21.6	4	-,1	-
I Meckiff	1	74	13	1	-,-	1
KD Mackay	0	40	14	4	-,-	-
R Benaud	4	86	23	3	-,-	-
JW Martin	0	37	8	1	-,-	-
RB Simpson	0	11	2	0	-,-	-

12th Men: FM Misson (Aus), PD Lashley (WI)

Umpires: CJ Egar, C Hoy

AUSTRALIA 1st Innings

Test #			Runs	Mins	4s,6s		Fall of Wickets				
42	CC McDonald	b Valentine	34	112	1,-		Wkt	fow	Runs	Mins	
9	RB Simpson	c Kanhai b Hall	10	23	0,-		1	17	17	23	Simpson / McDonald
68	RN Harvey	c Sobers b Hall	9	34	0,-		2	40	23	35	Harvey / McDonald
16	NC O'Neill	b Sobers	71	142	10,-		3	65	25	54	McDonald / O'Neill
18	LE Favell	c Worrell b Valentine	16	36	1,-		4	105	40	37	Favell / O'Neill
27	KD Mackay	c Solomon b Gibbs	39	134	2,-		5	155	50	52	O'Neill / Mackay
33	AK Davidson	c Worrell b Valentine	16	48	2,-		6	194	39	49	Davidson / Mackay
48,c20	R Benaud	c Valentine b Valentine	3	43	0,-		7	200	6	34	Mackay / Benaud
3	JW Martin	c Solomon b Gibbs	0	1	0,-		8	200	0	2	Martin / Benaud
20,w	ATW Grout	c Hunte b Gibbs	0	4	0,-		9	202	2	9	Grout / Benaud
17	I Meckiff	not out	0	3	0,-		10	202	0	3	Benaud / Meckiff
	Extras	b 1, lb 2, nb 1, w 0	4								
	Total	**74.2 overs All out**	**202**	**298**	**16,0**						

	Wkts	Runs	Ov	Mdns	nb,w	6s
WW Hall	2	53	13	0	1,-	-
FMM Worrell	0	18	9	4	-,-	-
LR Gibbs	3	46	23	6	-,-	-
AL Valentine	4	67	24.2	6	-,-	-
GStA Sobers	1	14	5	2	-,-	-

WEST INDIES 2nd Innings

		Runs		Mins	4s,6s	Match Runs		Fall of Wickets					
								Wkt	fow	Runs	Mins		
CC Hunte	c O'Neill b Davidson	1		20	0,-	35		1	10	10	20	Hunte / Smith	
CW Smith	c Simpson b Benaud	55		116	9,-	71		2	20	10	8	Kanhai / Smith	
RB Kanhai	c Martin b Davidson	3		7	0,-	24		3	22	2	11	Sobers / Smith	
GStA Sobers	c Grout b Davidson	1		10	0,-	169		4	123	101	77	Smith / Worrell	
FMM Worrell	lbw b Benaud	82		198	11,1	104		5	144	21	59	Nurse / Worrell	
SM Nurse	c Mackay b Mackay	11		58	0,-	54		6	159	15	26	Solomon / Worrell	
JS Solomon	c Harvey b Benaud	1		25	1,-	15		7	166	7	37	Worrell / Alexander	
FCM Alexander	lbw b Mackay	108		212	11,1	108		8	240	74	92	Gibbs / Alexander	
LR Gibbs	st Grout b Benaud	18		2	2,-	18		9	309	69	77	Hall / Alexander	
WW Hall	b Mackay	24		0	0,1	34		10	326	17	9	Alexander / Valentine	
AL Valentine	not out	10		2	2,-	10							
Extras	b 4, lb 7, nb 0, w 1	12				23							
Total	102.4 overs All out 326			417	36,2	665							

	Wkts		Runs	Ov	Mdns	nb,w	6s	Match				
AK Davidson	3		33	8	1	-,-	-		8	/	113	
R Benaud	4		113	44	14	-,-	1		8	/	199	
I Meckiff	0		12	5	2	-,-	-		1	/	86	
JW Martin	0		65	10	0	-,1	1		0	/	102	
KD Mackay	3		75	31.4	5	-,-	1		3	/	115	
RB Simpson	0		16	4	0	-,-	-		0	/	27	

AUSTRALIA 2nd Innings

		Runs	Mins	4s,6s	Match Runs		Fallof Wickets					
							Wkt	fow	Runs	Mins		
CC McDonald	c Alexander b Valentine	27	97	2,-	61		1	27	27	26	Simpson / McDonald	
RB Simpson	b Sobers	12	26	2,-	22		2	83	56	71	McDonald / Harvey	
RN Harvey	c Sobers b Gibbs	85	180	9,-	85		3	191	108	110	Harvey / O'Neill	
NC O'Neill	c Sobers b Gibbs	70	131	8,-	141		4	197	6	11	Favell / O'Neill	
LE Favell	b Gibbs	2	10	0,-	18		5	197	0	3	Mackay / O'Neill	
KD Mackay	c Nurse b Gibbs	0	2	0,-	39		6	202	5	8	O'Neill / Benaud	
R Benaud	c Valentine b Valentine	24	50	3,-	27		7	209	7	13	Martin / Benaud	
JW Martin	b Valentine	5	12	0,-	5		8	220	11	13	Grout / Benaud	
ATW Grout	b Gibbs	0	12	1,-	0		9	234	14	22	Benaud / Davidson	
AK Davidson	b Valentine	1	25	0,-	17		10	241	7	7	Davidson / Meckiff	
I Meckiff	not out	6	7	0,-	6							
Extras	b 3, lb 6, nb 0, w 0	9			13							
Total 72.2 overs All out		241	285	25,0	443							

	Wkts		Runs	Ov	Mdns	nb,w	6s	Match	
WW Hall	0		35	8	0	-,-	-	2/88	
GStA Sobers	1		38	9	1	-,-	-	2/52	
LR Gibbs	5		66	26	5	-,-	-	8/112	
AL Valentine	4		86	25.2	7	-,-	-	8/153	
FMM Worrell	0		7	4	0	-,-	-	0/25	

FOURTH TEST   ADELAIDE OVAL.

MATCH DRAWN.   **Toss: West Indies**

	Day	Close of play	Not out batsmen	Day runs	Day wkts	Day ov.	Day mins	Crowd
27-Jan-61	1	West Indies 7/348	Alexander 38, Gibbs 3	348	7	73	360	18,465
28-Jan-61	2	West Indies 393, Australia 4/221	Simpson 85, Benaud 1	266	7	76.5	342	23,561
30-Jan-61	3	Australia 366, West Indies 1/150	Hunte 44, Kanhai 59	295	7	80.6	364	35,072
31-Jan-61	4	West Indies 432, Australia 3/31	O'Neill 21	313	8	66.7	355	21,281
1-Feb-61	5	Australia 9/273		242	6	113	368	13,691
			TOTALS	**1464**	**35**	**410**	**1789**	**112,070**

WEST INDIES 1st Innings

Test #			Runs	Mins	4s,6s	Fall of Wickets				
20	CC Hunte	lbw b Hoare	6	14	1,-	Wkt	fow	Runs	Mins	
3	CW Smith	c Benaud b Benaud	28	80	3,-	1	12	12	14	Hunte / Smith
27	RB Kanhai	c Simpson b Benaud	117	149	14,2	2	83	71	66	Smith / Kanhai
36	GStA Sobers	b Benaud	1	8	0,-	3	91	8	9	Sobers / Kanhai
40,c4	FMM Worrell	c Misson b Hoare	71	174	10,-	4	198	107	75	Kanhai / Worrell
4	SM Nurse	c Misson b Misson	49	121	3,-	5	271	73	100	Worrell / Nurse
13	JS Solomon	c Benaud b Benaud	22	61	0,-	6	288	17	22	Nurse / Solomon
24,w	FCM Alexander	not out	63	148	5,-	7	316	28	40	Solomon / Alexander
10	LR Gibbs	b Misson	18	63	1,-	8	375	59	64	Gibbs / Alexander
17	WW Hall	c Hoare b Benaud	5	53	0,-	9	392	17	50	Alexander / Hall
33	AL Valentine	lbw b Misson	0	7	0,-	10	393	1	7	Hall / Valentine
	Extras	b 3, lb 3, nb 2, w 5	13							
	Total	**88.5 overs All out**	**393**	**438**	**37,2**					

	Wkts	Runs	Ov	Mdns	nb,w	6s	
DE Hoare	2	68	16	0	1,1	1	**12th Men: JW Martin (Aus), PD Lashley (WI)**
FM Misson	3	79	17.5	2	1,3	-	Umpires: CJ Egar, C Hoy
KD Mackay	0	11	2	0	-,-	-	
R Benaud	5	96	27	5	-,1	1	
LF Kline	0	109	21	3	-,-	-	
RB Simpson	0	17	5	0	-,-	-	

AUSTRALIA 1st Innings

Test #			Runs	Mins	4s,6s	Fall of Wickets				
43	CC McDonald	c Hunte b Gibbs	71	169	4,-	Wkt	fow	Runs	Mins	
19	LE Favell	c Alexander b Worrell	1	9	0,-	1	9	9	9	Favell / McDonald
17	NC O'Neill	c Alexander b Sobers	11	55	0,-	2	45	36	56	O'Neill / McDonald
10	RB Simpson	c Alexander b Hall	85	208	4,-	3	119	74	104	McDonald / Simpson
15	PJP Burge	b Sobers	45	92	5,-	4	213	94	93	Burge / Simpson
49,c21	R Benaud	c Solomon b Gibbs	77	213	7,-	5	221	8	12	Simpson / Benaud
28	KD Mackay	lbw b Gibbs	29	85	2,-	6	281	60	86	Mackay / Benaud
21,w	ATW Grout	c Sobers b Gibbs	0	1	0,-	7	281	0	2	Grout / Benaud
2	FM Misson	b Gibbs	0	1	0,-	8	281	0	2	Misson / Benaud
1	DE Hoare	b Sobers	35	104	2,-	9	366	85	111	Hoare / Benaud
13	LF Kline	not out	0	2	0,-	10	366	0	2	Benaud / Kline
	Extras	b 2, lb 3, nb 7, w 0	12							
	Total	**109.6 overs All out**	**366**	**478**	**24,0**					

	Wkts	Runs	Ov	Mdns	nb,w	6s
WW Hall	1	85	22	3	7,-	-
FMM Worrell	1	34	7	0	-,-	-
GStA Sobers	3	64	24	3	-,-	-
LR Gibbs	5	97	35.6	4	-,-	-
AL Valentine	0	74	21	4	-,-	-

WEST INDIES 2nd Innings

		Runs	Mins	4s,6s	Match Runs	Fall of Wickets				
						Wkt	fow	Runs	Mins	
CC Hunte	run out	79	220	6,-	85	1	66	66	61	Smith / Hunte
CW Smith	c Hoare b Mackay	46	61	10,-	74	2	229	163	159	Hunte / Kanhai
RB Kanhai	lbw b Benaud	115	222	12,-	232	3	263	34	64	Kanhai / Sobers
GStA Sobers	run out	20	79	1,-	21	4	270	7	16	Sobers / Worrell
FMM Worrell	c Burge b Mackay	53	136	8,-	124	5	275	5	14	Nurse / Worrell
SM Nurse	c Simpson b Benaud	5	13	1,-	54	6	388	113	107	Worrell / Alexander
FCM Alexander	not out	87	148	10,-	150	7		44*	41	Solomon / Alexander
JS Solomon	not out	16	40	1,-	38					
Extras	b 2, lb 6, nb 1, w 2	11			24					
Total	92 overs 6 wkts decl.	432	465	49,0	825					

	Wkts	Runs	Ov	Mdns	nb,w	6s	Match
DE Hoare	0	88	13	0	1,1	-	2/156
FM Misson	0	106	28	3	-,-	-	3/185
R Benaud	2	107	27	3	-,-	-	7/203
KD Mackay	2	72	12	0	-,-	-	2/83
LF Kline	0	48	12	2	-,1	-	0/157

AUSTRALIA 2nd Innings

		Runs	Mins	4s,6s	Match Runs	Fall of Wickets				
						Wkt	fow	Runs	Mins	
CC McDonald	run out	2	20	0,-	73	1	6	6	12	Favell / McDonald
LE Favell	c Alexander b Hall	4	12	1,-	5	2	7	1	8	McDonald / O'Neill
NC O'Neill	c Sobers b Sobers	65	179	8,-	76	3	31	24	19	Simpson / O'Neill
RB Simpson	c Alexander b Hall	3	18	0,-	3	4	113	82	100	Burge / O'Neill
PJP Burge	c Alexander b Valentine	49	99	5,-	94	5	129	16	53	O'Neill / Benaud
R Benaud	c Sobers b Sobers	17	61	2,-	94	6	144	15	9	Benaud / Mackay
KD Mackay	not out	62	223	6,-	91	7	203	59	77	Grout / Mackay
ATW Grout	lbw b Worrell	42	76	5,-	42	8	207	4	15	Misson / Mackay
FM Misson	c Solomon b Worrell	1	14	0,-	1	9	207	0	13	Hoare / Mackay
DE Hoare	b Worrell	0	3	0,-	35	10		66*	109	Mackay / Kline
LF Kline	not out	15	109	2,-	15					
Extras	b 9, lb 1, nb 3, w 0	13			25					
Total	120 overs All out	273	408	29,0	639					

	Wkts	Runs	Ov	Mdns	nb,w	6s	Match
WW Hall	2	61	13	4	3,-	-	3/146
GStA Sobers	2	87	39	1	-,-	-	5/151
LR Gibbs	0	44	28	3	-,-	-	5/141
AL Valentine	1	40	20	7	-,-	-	1/114
JS Solomon	0	1	3	2	-,-	-	0/1
FMM Worrell	3	27	17	9	-,-	-	4/61

FIFTH TEST — MELBOURNE CRICKET GROUND.

AUSTRALIA WON BY 2 WICKETS.   **Toss: Australia**

	Day	Close of play	Not out batsmen	Day runs	Day wkts	Day ov.	Day mins	Crowd
10-Feb-61	1	West Indies 8/252	Solomon 21, Hall 5	252	8	76	325	46,225
11-Feb-61	2	West Indies 292, Australia 3/236	Burge 37, Mackay 16	276	5	94.7	388	90,800
13-Feb-61	3	Australia 356, West Indies 2/126	Hunte 46, Solomon 9	246	9	76.4	349	51,391
14-Feb-61	4	West Indies 321, Australia 1/57	Simpson 44, Benaud 1	252	9	74.7	344	44,822
15-Feb-61	5	Australia 8/258		201	7	96.7	310	41,186
			TOTALS	**1227**	**38**	**419**	**1716**	**274,424**

WEST INDIES 1st Innings

Test #				Runs	Mins	4s,6s	Fall of Wickets				
4	CW Smith	c O'Neill b Misson		11	32	1,-	Wkt	fow	Runs	Mins	
21	CC Hunte	c Simpson b Davidson		31	136	4,-	1	18	18	32	Smith / Hunte
28	RB Kanhai	c Harvey b Benaud		38	76	7,-	2	75	57	77	Kanhai / Hunte
37	GStA Sobers	c Grout b Simpson		64	177	5,-	3	81	6	27	Hunte / Sobers
41,c5	FMM Worrell	c Grout b Martin		10	40	0,-	4	107	26	41	Worrell / Sobers
2	PD Lashley	c Misson b Benaud		41	99	4,-	5	200	93	100	Lashley / Sobers
25,w	FCM Alexander	c McDonald b Misson		11	42	1,-	6	204	4	10	Sobers / Alexander
14	JS Solomon	run out		45	141	3,-	7	221	17	33	Alexander / Solomon
11	LR Gibbs	c Burge b Misson		11	14	1,-	8	235	14	15	Gibbs / Solomon
18	WW Hall	b Misson		21	84	1,-	9	290	55	84	Hall / Solomon
34	AL Valentine	not out		0	6	0,-	10	292	2	6	Solomon / Valentine
	Extras	b 4, lb 4, nb 0, w 1		9							
	Total	**89.7 overs All out**		**292**	**431**	**23,0**					

	Wkts	Runs	Ov	Mdns	nb,w	6s
AK Davidson	1	89	27	4	-,-	-
FM Misson	4	58	14	3	-,1	-
KD Mackay	0	1	1	0	-,-	-
R Benaud	2	55	21.7	5	-,-	-
JW Martin	1	29	8	0	-,-	-
RB Simpson	1	51	18	3	-,-	-

12th Men: LF Kline (Aus), CD Watson (WI)

Umpires: CJ Egar, C Hoy

AUSTRALIA 1st Innings

Test #				Runs	Mins	4s,6s	Fall of Wickets				
11	RB Simpson	c Gibbs b Sobers		75	200	5,-	Wkt	fow	Runs	Mins	
44	CC McDonald	lbw b Sobers		91	166	6,-	1	146	146	166	McDonald / Simpson
18	NC O'Neill	b Gibbs		10	34	0,-	2	181	35	34	Simpson / O'Neill
16	PJP Burge	c Sobers b Gibbs		68	194	7,-	3	181	0	1	O'Neill / Burge
29	KD Mackay	c Alexander b Hall		19	95	1,-	4	244	63	96	Mackay / Burge
69	RN Harvey	c Alexander b Sobers		5	26	0,-	5	260	16	27	Harvey / Burg
34	AK Davidson	c Alexander b Sobers		24	69	1,-	6	309	49	70	Davidson / Burge
50,c22	R Benaud	b Gibbs		3	21	0,-	7	309	0	1	Burge / Benaud
4	JW Martin	c Kanhai b Sobers		15	42	1,-	8	319	10	21	Benaud / Martin
3	FM Misson	not out		12	54	1,-	9	335	16	28	Martin / Misson
22,w	ATW Grout	c Hunte b Gibbs		14	28	0,-	10	356	21	28	Grout / Misson
	Extras	b 4, lb 8, nb 8, w 0		20							
	Total	**121.4 overs All out**		**356**	**473**	**22,0**					

	Wkts	Runs	Ov	Mdns	nb,w	6s
WW Hall	1	56	15	1	8,-	-
FMM Worrell	0	44	11	2	-,-	-
GStA Sobers	5	120	44	7	-,-	-
AL Valentine	0	42	13	3	-,-	-
LR Gibbs	4	74	38.4	18	-,-	-

WEST INDIES 2nd Innings

		Runs	Mins	4s,6s	Match Runs		Fall of Wickets				
							Wkt	fow	Runs	Mins	
CW Smith	lbw b Davidson	37	61	5,1	48		1	54	54	61	Smith / Hunte
CC Hunte	c Grout b Davidson	52	179	4,-	83		2	103	49	56	Kanhai / Hunte
RB Kanhai	c Misson b Benaud	31	55	4,-	69		3	135	32	62	Hunte / Solomon
JS Solomon	run out	36	162	3,-	81		4	173	38	62	Sobers / Solomon
GStA Sobers	c Grout b Simpson	21	61	1,-	85		5	201	28	39	Solomon / Alexander
FCM Alexander	c Mackay b Davidson	73	155	5,-	84		6	218	17	22	Worrell / Alexander
FMM Worrell	c Grout b Davidson	7	21	1,-	17		7	262	44	46	Lashley / Alexander
PD Lashley	lbw b Martin	18	45	1,-	59		8	295	33	49	Alexander / Gibbs
LR Gibbs	c O'Neill b Simpson	8	54	1,-	19		9	304	9	15	Gibbs / Hall
WW Hall	c Grout b Davidson	21	34	2,-	42		10	321	17	19	Hall / Valentine
AL Valentine	not out	3	19	0,-	3						
Extras	b 5, lb 8, nb 0, w 1	14			23						
Total	**95.7 overs All out**	**321**	**436**	**27,1**	**613**						

	Wkts	Runs	Ov	Mdns	nb,w	6s	Match
AK Davidson	5	84	24.7	4	-,-	-	6/173
FM Misson	0	58	10	1	-,-	1	4/116
RB Simpson	2	55	18	4	-,1	-	3/106
R Benaud	1	53	23	4	-,-	-	3/108
KD Mackay	0	21	10	2	-,-	-	0/22
JW Martin	1	36	10	1	-,-	-	2/65

AUSTRALIA 2nd Innings

		Runs	Mins	4s,6s	Match Runs		Fall of Wickets				
							Wkt	fow	Runs	Mins	
RB Simpson	b Gibbs	92	194	10,-	167		1	50	50	53	McDonald / Simpson
CC McDonald	c Smith b Gibbs	11	53	0,-	102		2	75	25	43	Benaud / Simpson
R Benaud	b Valentine	6	42	0,-	9		3	154	79	98	Simpson / O'Neill
NC O'Neill	c Alexander b Worrell	48	145	5,-	58		4	176	22	48	O'Neill / Burge
PJP Burge	b Valentine	53	155	8,-	121		5	200	24	40	Harvey / Burge
RN Harvey	c Smith b Worrell	12	39	1,-	12		6	236	36	49	Davidson / Burge
AK Davidson	c Sobers b Worrell	12	48	1,-	36		7	248	12	19	Burge / Mackay
KD Mackay	not out	3	42	0,-	22		8	256	8	11	Grout / Mackay
ATW Grout	c Smith b Valentine	5	10	0,-	19		9		2*	12	Martin / Mackay
JW Martin	not out	1	3	0,-	16						
Extras	b 3, lb 9, nb 3, w 0	15			35						
Total	**111.7 overs 8 wkts**	**258**	**377**	**25,0**	**614**						

	Wkts	Runs	Ov	Mdns	nb,w	6s	Match
WW Hall	0	40	5	0	3,-	-,1	/ 106
GStA Sobers	0	32	13	2	-,-	-,5	/ 152
FMM Worrell	3	43	31	6	-,-	-,3	/ 87
LR Gibbs	2	68	41	9	-,-	-,6	/ 142
AL Valentine	3	60	21.7	4	-,-	-,3	/ 102

TEST CAREER AVERAGES

AUSTRALIA

BATTING	Debut	M	Inn	NO	Runs	H.S	50	100	Avrge	Ct/St
Benaud, R	1951-52	63	97	7	2201	122	9	3	24.46	65
Burge, PJP	1954-55	42	68	8	2290	181	12	4	38.17	23
Davidson, AK	1953	44	61	7	1328	80	5	0	24.59	42
Favell, LE	1954-55	19	31	3	757	101	5	1	27.04	9
Grout, ATW	1957-58	51	67	8	890	74	3	0	15.08	163/24
Harvey, RN	1947-48	79	137	10	6149	205	24	21	48.42	64
Hoare, DE	1960-61	1	2	0	35	35	0	0	17.50	2
Kline, LF	1957-58	13	16	9	58	15*	0	0	8.29	9
Mackay, KD	1956	37	52	7	1507	89	13	0	33.49	16
Martin, JW	1960-61	8	13	1	214	55	1	0	17.83	5
McDonald, CC	1951-52	47	83	4	3107	170	17	5	39.33	14
Meckiff, I	1957-58	18	20	7	154	45*	0	0	11.85	9
Misson, FM	1960-61	5	5	3	38	25*	0	0	19.00	6
O'Neill, NC	1958-59	42	69	8	2779	181	15	6	45.56	21
Simpson, RB	1957-58	62	111	7	4869	311	27	10	46.82	110

AUSTRALIA

BOWLING	Balls	Mdns	Runs	Wkts	Avrge	5w/i	10w/m	Best
Benaud, R	19108	805	6704	248	27.03	16	1	7/72
Burge, PJP	-	-	-	-	-	-	-	-
Davidson, AK	11587	431	3819	186	20.53	14	2	7/93
Favell, LE	-	-	-	-	-	-	-	-
Grout, ATW	-	-	-	-	-	-	-	-
Harvey, RN	414	23	120	3	40.00	0	0	1/8
Hoare, DE	232	0	156	2	78.00	0	0	2/68
Kline, LF	2373	113	776	34	22.82	1	0	7/75
Mackay, KD	5792	267	1721	50	34.42	2	0	6/42
Martin, JW	1846	57	832	17	48.94	0	0	3/56
McDonald, CC	8	0	3	0	-	-	-	-
Meckiff, I	3734	120	1423	45	31.62	2	0	6/38
Misson, FM	1197	30	616	16	38.50	0	0	4/58
O'Neill, NC	1392	48	667	17	39.24	0	0	4/41
Simpson, RB	6881	253	3001	71	42.27	2	0	5/57

TEST CAREER AVERAGES

WEST INDIES

BATTING	Debut	M	Inn	NO	Runs	H.S	50	100	Avrge	Ct/St
Alexander, FCM	1957	25	38	6	961	108	7	1	30.03	85/5
Gibbs, LR	1957-58	79	109	39	488	25	0	0	6.97	52
Hall, WW	1958-59	48	66	14	818	50*	2	0	15.73	11
Hunte, CC	1957-58	44	78	6	3245	260	13	8	45.07	16
Kanhai, RB	1957	79	137	6	6227	256	28	15	47.53	50
Lashley, PD	1960-61	4	7	0	159	49	0	0	22.71	4
Nurse, SM	1959-60	29	54	1	2523	258	10	6	47.60	21
Ramadhin, S	1950	43	58	14	361	44	0	0	8.20	9
Smith, CW	1960-61	5	10	1	222	55	1	0	24.67	4/1
Sobers, GS	1953-54	93	160	21	8032	365*	30	26	57.78	109
Solomon, JS	1958-59	27	46	7	1326	100*	9	1	34.00	13
Valentine, AL	1950	36	51	21	141	14	0	0	4.70	13
Watson, CD	1959-60	7	6	1	12	5	0	0	2.40	1
Worrell, FMM	1947-48	51	87	9	3860	261	22	9	49.49	43

WEST INDIES

BOWLING	Balls	Mdns	Runs	Wkts	Avrge	5w/i	10w/m	Best
Alexander, FCM	-	-	-	-	-	-	-	-
Gibbs, LR	27115	1313	8989	309	29.09	18	2	8/38
Hall, WW	10421	312	5066	192	26.39	9	1	7/69
Hunte, CC	270	11	110	2	55.00	0	0	1/17
Kanhai, RB	183	8	85	0	-	0	0	-
Lashley, PD	18	2	1	1	1.00	0	0	1/1
Nurse, SM	42	4	7	0	-	0	0	-
Ramadhin, S	13939	813	4579	158	28.98	10	1	7/49
Smith, CW	-	-	-	-	-	-	-	-
Sobers, GS	21599	974	7999	235	34.04	6	0	6/73
Solomon, JS	702	39	268	4	67.00	0	0	1/20
Valentine, AL	12953	789	4215	139	30.32	8	2	8/104
Watson, CD	1458	47	724	19	38.11	0	0	4/62
Worrell, FMM	7141	274	2672	69	38.72	2	0	7/70